2nd Edition

Passing Exams

FOR

DUMMIES

A Wiley Brand

by Patrick Sherratt

FOR

DUMMIES

A Wiley Brand

Passing Exams For Dummies®

2nd Edition published by
Wiley Publishing Australia Pty Ltd
42 McDougall Street
Milton, Qld 4064
www.dummies.com

Copyright © 2014 Wiley Publishing Australia Pty Ltd

The moral rights of the author have been asserted.

National Library of Australia
Cataloguing-in-Publication data:

Author:	Sherratt, Patrick, 1970 –
Title:	Passing Exams For Dummies / Patrick Sherratt
Edition:	2nd edition
ISBN:	9780730304425 (pbk.)
Notes:	Includes index.
Series:	For Dummies.
Subjects:	Examinations — Study guides
	Test-taking skills
Dewey Number:	371.30281

Cover image: © iStockphoto.com/kristian sekulic

Typeset by diacriTech, Chennai, India

Printed in Singapore by
C.O.S. Printers Pte Ltd

10 9 8 7 6 5 4 3 2 1

Contents at a Glance

Table of Contents

Introduction

*I*n school, I under-achieved and my exam grades showed it. As a teenager I didn't really know what I wanted to do when I left school. I knew what I didn't want to do — go to a university! My parents didn't go; my older brother and sister didn't go, so going to college never really entered my head. With no clear goals, I floated through school doing enough to get through, but never aiming to excel. A decade later, standing in the unemployment line because the company I'd been working for had gone bust, I realized that I needed to go back to school.

As an adult student in college, I wanted to do well academically. I studied psychology and education, and in the process of taking a lot of tests, became interested in finding out how examinations measure learning. As I researched and applied how to improve learning and how to prepare for exams, I started to do very well in school. For the first time in my life, I was getting As and Bs. One year, I won an award for excellence. My confidence soared and my academic self-image improved — I was smarter than I once thought.

Are you taking an exam soon? Let me assure you: After you discover how your brain functions; how your thinking influences your learning; how your memory works; and then synthesize this kind of meta-cognitive knowledge into a practical step-by-step approach to preparing for exams, you can make huge improvements to your exam results. I did, and I'm convinced that doing well isn't necessarily about how naturally smart you are academically, but about how smart you are in your preparation techniques.

So why are you holding this book? Are you a senior wanting to get through high school, or a college or university student going for a degree? Perhaps you're in a life transition and returning to education to gain new skills, or you're about to take a career exam to improve your chances of a promotion? Whatever your reason for picking up this book on passing exams, achieving academic success is possible when you know how.

Be aware. Words don't teach; experience teaches. The information contained in this book is absolutely meaningless unless you're prepared to incorporate it into your current exam preparation.

So, you have a decision to make. How badly do you want to pass your exams? Are you prepared to do the work and apply the ideas in this book? If not, put this book down right now and walk away. You'll find no value here unless you're willing to explore different parts of this book and use the exercises to improve your exam preparation skills.

About This Book

I've devoted a lot of time and effort over the years to implementing different learning strategies for students, based on my Masters in Education research and personal trial and error. In this book, my intention is to connect with students like you, and give you the best ways I know to improve your exam preparation and ultimately your performance. You can avoid making the same mistake I made in high school; you can take advantage of my years of research and exam experiences and apply these ideas immediately.

In *Passing Exams For Dummies*, 2nd Edition, you can start reading anywhere you want to. The book's modular format means that instead of reading from cover to cover, you can dip in and get the how-to information you need. This is a great time-saving feature — and believe me, I know all about saving time. When you have a mountain of reading to do for exams, the last thing you want to read is another book!

Consider this book a study guide waiting to offer you some well-researched, good advice on how to better prepare for your next exam. Do this and you'll ultimately save time!

I deliberately tried to make this book easy to read by using simple language. I use the following conventions to help information stand out:

- When I introduce a new concept, I *italicize* the term, then provide a definition.

- I show website addresses in a different font so they're easy to identify — just type the address as it appears in the book and you'll go straight to the site. And, if the URL breaks to the next line, I don't add a hyphen, so type in exactly what you see.

If you're interested in saving time (like me), you can bypass some information in this book, which I put in simply to please the publisher, otherwise the book looks too thin (just kidding!). For example, occasionally I explain a technical term, especially when covering how your brain works. These paragraphs are accompanied by a Technical Stuff icon, and you can skip them if you want. Similarly, the Patrick Says icon highlights paragraphs that offer personal experiences you may find interesting, but they're not vital reading.

I've also thrown in some fun exercises in the sidebars — those shaded boxes you see in many chapters. You can skip these too; however, I'm hoping you find them intriguing.

Foolish Assumptions

Exams are not something people do for fun, but they're necessary as long as education systems use the current assessment paradigm. (Although many people believe exams should be done away with, I would be out of a job if that were the case.) So, I assume you have a genuine purpose for reading this book, which may be any one of the following — or a combination of several:

- ✔ You'll be undertaking exams in the near future and you're looking for some basic guidelines and quick tips to help you improve your chances of passing them or doing better than before.

- ✔ You're interested in the how-to of good exam preparation but want the minimum amount of theory.

- ✔ You want to feel confident that you're making the best use of your study time because your time is precious.

- ✔ You may have not done so well on exams in the past and want to improve your overall performance.

- ✔ A long time has passed since you last studied and you want to ensure your success.

- ✔ Passing these exams is really important to you and you're serious about applying these ideas to maximize your results.

Icons Used in This Book

Use the icons in the margins of this book to pinpoint the information you desire. The meaning for each icon is explained here:

Where to find interesting information on a website that puts you in touch with further resources on preparing for exams.

Although not vital reading, this icon highlights interesting stories from my own and other people's experiences.

This icon indicates important stuff to store away in your memory. You could circle these icons as you read chapters in this book.

This icon marks extra technical information that you don't need as such, but provides interesting details. Read and enjoy, or give the information a miss if you like.

This handy little icon flags special things that can help you to improve your exam preparation. They're little gems of information that can help you make the most of the time you spend studying.

Stop! Watch out! This icon flags common mistakes students make — or what you need to be wary of when you're preparing for and taking exams.

Beyond the Book

In addition to the material in the print or ebook you're reading right now, *Passing Exams For Dummies*, 2nd Edition, also comes with some access-anywhere goodies on the Web. Check out the free Cheat Sheet at www.dummies.com/cheatsheet/passingexams for some quick action steps you can use to turn your preparation into improved results. The online Cheat Sheet will help you feel confident in knowing that the time you do spend preparing for your exams is used in the best possible way. For the latest updates on other companion material for this book, visit www.dummies.com/go/passingexamsfd.

Where to Go from Here

I have absolutely no doubt the information in this book can help you improve your exam performance! If you're facing your first exam, check out the chapters in Part I for ways to develop your exam performance mindset. If you have trouble remembering pertinent information, go to Part IV for some tips. Or, if you want to cover all the bases, read this book in sequence, especially the practical steps included in Parts II to V.

After your exams are over, that's it. You can place this book on the shelf to gather dust until your next exams. It's simply a tool to help you improve a certain aspect of your academic life. In the meantime, use the tool wisely. Write in it, scribble in it, tag or dog-ear pages for future reference — do whatever you can to get the best use out of this book.

Finally, I wish you well through your examination process and sincerely hope you can apply these powerful ideas to help you prepare and pass your exams with ease. Go well.

Part I

Releasing Your Potential to Pass Exams

getting started with

passing your exams

Visit www.dummies.com for great (and free!) Dummies content online.

In this part ...

- ✔ Find out how your brain works and explore the mechanics of what happens in your brain when you are learning and studying for exams.

- ✔ Discover key principles to get your brain switched on and working to improve how you review, retain, and recall information.

- ✔ Explore your ideal learning states and styles to help make learning and study easier.

- ✔ Get essential tips on how to keep motivated, manage your study time, and concentrate effectively.

- ✔ Understand how your mind works and how to harness the power of an *exam performance mindset* to improve your preparation and ultimately your results.

Chapter 1

Passing Exams: Preparation Is Everything!

*H*ave you ever thought of taking a test as giving a performance? If you're into music, sports, or drama then you already know the benefits of thinking this way: Preparing beforehand improves your abilities, so that when you get to the podium, the field, or the stage, you can give your best performance.

You can approach exams the same way. During an exam you sit at a desk for several hours, concentrating and writing as fast as you can. Your preparation beforehand determines how well you perform in the exam.

In this chapter, I help you gain an understanding of where you are right now with regard to your exam performance mindset. This understanding can help you develop strategies to enhance your thinking and use techniques that enable you to perform at your peak on exam day.

Developing Your Exam Performance Mindset

No matter what subjects you're studying, whether you're in high school, in college, at university, or facing vocational or entrance exams, to pass your exams you need to do these things:

- ✔ Attend classes, pay attention, and make notes for later review.

  Teachers only present information — they don't put it in your head. That's your task and, usually, you're required to follow up with research or further reading.

- ✔ Organize your class notes and plan your study time.

- ✔ Become well acquainted with the subject matter. This involves improving your ability to study and to retain information — two different skill-sets. Right now, you may simply call it study, but to answer exam questions you need to know how to retain information and access it when you need it.

- ✔ Demonstrate your knowledge by performing well on the exam. If you don't perform well on the exam, your results won't reflect how well you know the subject.

Obviously, accomplishing all this takes work, and developing an exam performance mindset gives you a good start and helps you

- ✔ Maintain an attitude of excellence.

- ✔ Know very clearly what you want and why you want to pass your exams (which is your goal, after all).

- ✔ Identify and address how and why you may be holding yourself back.

With the right mindset, you can discover your capabilities, clarify your motives, and gain a better understanding of yourself. Learning and studying then become much easier — and fun!

Cultivating the right attitude

The famous Greek philosopher Aristotle said, "We are what we repeatedly do. Excellence, then, is not an act, but a habit." What he meant is that the quality and quantity of your thinking determine how your life goes. If your predominant thoughts are affirming, positive, constructive, and generally optimistic, the quality of your decisions, actions, and ultimately what happens to you will be great as well.

Think about whether your thoughts drive you forward towards being the best you can or make you feel defeated before you've even started.

All meaningful and lasting change begins on the inside, then slowly becomes a reality. Change involves addressing your thinking processes. Becoming aware of what you're telling yourself on the inside helps bring constructive, affirming, positive thoughts to the forefront of your mind. Through repetition, you can make them a habit. You can train your subconscious mind so that you naturally perform at your best no matter what you're doing.

Setting your purpose

Sailing through life without purpose is like sailing the oceans without a destination. A rogue sailor's life may interest some people, but a successful career requires direction. To do well in exams you need to know very clearly *why* you want to achieve good results (or, what you want to do next).

I didn't do very well in my high school exams, mainly because I had no clear-set academic goals and therefore no real reason why I should pass. I didn't know what I was going to do when I left school, so it didn't matter to me how well I did.

The trick is deciding what you want, and then deciding why you want it. Take a moment to visualize achieving your exam goals, then explore all the benefits that follow. Clarifying your purpose in this way helps maintain your motivation when the going gets tough — and when exam time rolls round and you have more than one test to prepare for, the going will get tough!

Clearing roadblocks

Sometimes you may consciously choose a goal (for example, to pass an exam so that you're qualified to do a job you've been offered), but for some reason, you unconsciously sabotage a good outcome. Perhaps you're beset by self-defeating, critical thoughts that point out why you won't do as well in the exam as you hope. Or you may procrastinate, putting your preparation off until the last minute, then discover you need more time. The small amount of reviewing you do is inefficient and leads to a poor result.

The way around problems like self-defeating thoughts is to identify and analyze all the reasons you may be trying to hinder your own progress. Listing what you perceive to be lacking in your knowledge or skills helps you pinpoint your negative attitudes and beliefs. This requires digging deep and being honest with yourself.

When you become aware of the ways you limit yourself, you can take steps to rectify your behavior so that you're not working against your goals — when it comes to exams or anything else. You can then identify and analyze your good qualities and strengths, and discover reasons why you *can* have what you want. Focusing on good qualities and strengths also improves your motivation because you have a higher expectation of success.

Exploring your layers — just like Shrek

If you saw the first *Shrek* movie, you may remember the scene where he was talking to Donkey about the onion analogy. What the onion analogy says is that everyone has many layers, which define who they are. However, people usually see only the outer layers (your facade), which may not be who you think and feel you really are, or who you could be. You can peel back the outer layers if you want and discover where your true potential lies.

To develop an exam performance mindset, you have to peel back those layers and identify the ones that are holding you back, and then bring to the fore the layers that can drive you forward. Sometimes, however, the people closest to you may not like to see changes in you and can hold you back. They've known your outer layers for so long that when you try to show an inner layer — a new way of being — they become disturbed because they're unfamiliar with your new behavior.

It takes courage and support to show your deeper layers. By surrounding yourself with higher performing friends — people who can support your expression of new layers — you'll find that their expectations of you can help you realize your full potential.

Understanding Your Brain's Capabilities

Just as top singers need to know how their lungs and throat muscles work in order to reach high, rich notes, understanding how your brain works enables you to think more clearly and retain information. Knowing how your brain drives your thinking is the foundation on which you build your exam performance mindset.

You probably already know that your brain has many physical aspects and functions, and that when you learn something new, brain cells develop, connect, and communicate to each other. Recent discoveries (which scientists are just beginning to understand) show that the human brain has amazing adaptability, called *neuroplasticity*, and can change to cater to the demands you place on it when you learn something new. Also, the link between emotion and memory retention is now better understood and shows that you learn better when you're curious, surprised, or having fun — experiencing any positive emotional experience.

In Chapter 2, I explain how your brain works, and how you can develop areas of your brain that use specific thinking processes if they're lacking and causing you to under-perform in specific subjects. I also explore your brain's capability to block out, or let in, information based on whether the information is of interest or value.

For example, if you tell yourself that a subject is boring, it has no value for you, and your brain's attention system is less likely to allow the information to be processed because it will be paying attention to something you judge as more important. Finding value and setting goals are key to getting your brain's attention switched on. Exploring your attitudes to learning allows you to find value in the topic you're studying. These factors are intrinsic to developing your exam performance mindset. I talk more about finding value and setting goals in Chapter 4.

Relaxation also plays a role in making your brain receptive to learning — turn to Chapter 6 for some great reasons why I think you should go to the beach or take a walk in the park. When you're relaxed as opposed to feeling stressed or tense, your brainwaves slow down to an amplitude and frequency that allows brain cells to more easily absorb information (see Chapter 5). Even doing a simple relaxation exercise before a study session helps your brain to be more receptive to the information you're presenting it. (Appendix B has a relaxation script you can try out.)

Your brain is an organ that needs maintenance and nourishment. Looking after your brain while you're studying is especially important, because learning relies on brain cell processes. Good nutrition, drinking plenty of water, and supplying your brain with extra oxygen through exercise all improve transmission between brain cells. Activities like juggling and exercises for your brain, which I cover in Chapter 2, help brain cell development too.

Looking at Ideal Ways to Learn

As you go through school and your chosen career(s), you're required to incorporate new information and procedures quickly and seamlessly. Knowing how you learn best, coupled with a practical step-by-step approach for assimilating information, is useful not only now but throughout your life.

Learning is a complex task, and everyone has individual differences that govern the way they process information in the brain. In Chapter 3, I step you through primary learning styles and thinking patterns, and show you how to address your weaker learning styles. I also help you discover and implement techniques to improve how well and quickly you learn. These techniques enhance your exam performance mindset and involve

- ✔ Identifying your ideal study environment (this includes finding ways to reduce distractions).
- ✔ Being aware of your natural body rhythms and alertness cycles — your best times for learning.
- ✔ Understanding how to increase your motivation, including how to develop and maintain your concentration.
- ✔ Developing and sticking to a timetable to manage your review and study time.

Understanding your learning and thinking styles — how your brain prefers to process and communicate information — allows you to match review techniques to the way you learn best. This saves you time. (I show you which methods are best in Chapter 14.)

Enhancing Your Thinking Processes

Knowing where to start with modifying your exam preparation techniques to improve your performance may seem hard. Sometimes you get a clear sense that you understand how your mind works and can easily apply yourself to a task. At other times you have the general feeling that you've stepped out of your comfort zone, feel anxious, and lack motivation. You understand what you need to do, then find you behave a different way.

In Chapter 4, I explain how thinking processes work and why many of the thoughts that run your life are mostly based on your nonconscious memory. You have conscious and nonconscious thinking processes, but you're only consciously aware of some of your perceptions and behaviors.

Your conscious *mind* perceives, associates, and evaluates information based on your past conditioning — drawing on your attitudes, beliefs, and habits of thought. Most of the decisions you make today are based on past experiences, and these are stored in your memory. Your memory holds your *personal truth* — your real assessment of yourself — and automatically works to maintain your truth. Academically, and in all other areas of your life, you respond to situations from a belief level, not a potential level. If your attitudes and beliefs about your academic ability in a particular subject are limiting, you self-regulate your thinking and behavior to keep you at that level.

High achievers imprint their memory deliberately to enhance their exam performance. You, too, can get your memory working for you instead of against you. The first step is to listen to your *self-talk* — the conversations you have with yourself in your head — for any limiting ideas you may have about your ability to learn something new. These thoughts influence your self-images, which regulate your performance.

Start seeing yourself reaching higher academic standards. Ways to do this include gathering information from students who are already performing at the level you want to perform. Interview them and find out how they think and what they do to prepare for their exams. If you start conditioning yourself to think and behave in the same way, your results will rise to higher levels. Rehearsing your ideal exam, covered in Chapter 15, also imprints your memory, and plays a key role in improving how you perform on exam day.

Another thinking strategy that enhances academic performance is setting high academic goals. Set your goals just ahead of your current capabilities and ensure the higher level is the most dominant picture in your mind. As I explain in Chapter 4, this gets imprinted into your memory as truth, allowing you to think creatively and solve problems.

So how do you make your goals the most dominant pictures in your mind? Through repeating *affirmations* — deliberate, positive self-talk. Repeated often, affirmations imprint on your memory. If you combine affirmations with visualization and associated feelings, you can engage your mind to work with you towards your goals, rather than allow it to hold you back through limiting attitudes, procrastination, and poor effort. (Chapter 4 tells you how to compose effective affirmations.)

Effective Exam Preparation

In this section, I narrow down effective exam preparation to four practical steps you can undertake, in sequence, the moment you sit down to review for a test. Combined with an exam performance mindset, this logical step-by-step approach can help you feel confident that you're making the best use of your time.

Factoring in relaxation

When you're stressed, anxious, or uptight, your brain and memory don't easily engage. Relaxing helps prime your brain to be ready and receptive to remembering the material you review. In Chapter 6, I offer you many ways to relax, and include practical suggestions to help you organize your time more efficiently.

Relaxing before any study session also helps get your brain in the ideal state for learning. When you relax, your brainwaves slow down, making your brain cells more receptive to processing and storing information (as I explain fully in Chapter 5).

Studying with purpose

One of the keys to an effective review is to set your intent or purpose on what you want to achieve during the study session (see Chapter 7). After you relax, you tell your brain what's important to review. In other words, defining your intent or purpose stimulates your awareness to be particular about what information is important and what information is not.

With your intent set, you can begin reviewing your class notes. But where should you begin? A good starting point is using advice offered by teachers and looking at past exam papers, as I outline in Chapter 8. You can then organize your notes for review by

- ✔ **Skim reading:** When you feel confident you're studying the right content, begin with *skim reading* your notes. This means taking a moment to look at an introduction or summary, first sentences in a paragraph, and any pictures with captions. This is a priming technique, because your brain can't comprehend something it doesn't recognize. When you skim read, you give your brain something to associate with later.

- ✔ **Study reading:** You use this review technique (described fully in Chapter 9) to gain understanding of the material while simultaneously looking for keywords or key concepts that represent large chunks of information. The idea is that if you could pull out one word and remember that word, you would be able to remember that entire chunk of information. You're looking for ways to condense large amounts of information into keywords.

- ✔ **Visual formats:** People think and remember better through pictures and patterns. Turning all your condensed notes into visual cues helps you remember information more easily. Mind mapping, creating concept maps, and writing essay route maps, covered in Chapter 10, make great visual aids — and software is available to help you produce them.

Boosting your memory with pictures and patterns

In a nutshell, the different ways you can study to enhance memory retention are

- ✔ Setting your intention to improve your attention, concentration, and motivation.
- ✔ Creating keyword pictures or patterns from your information.
- ✔ Making your keyword pictures exaggerated, unusual, or emotional.
- ✔ Making your keyword pictures active by imagining them moving.
- ✔ Associating your keyword pictures with familiar objects.
- ✔ Repeatedly rehearsing your keyword pictures to ensure retention.

In Chapter 11, I explore how your memory works and how you can improve your retention when revising for exams. I show you memorizing techniques, beginning with basic methods in Chapter 12 and introduce advanced memorizing techniques in Chapter 13.

Rehearsing for recall and your best on-the-day performance

Rehearsing for recall and rehearsing your ideal exam performance in your mind are two very important aspects of studying for an exam. Practicing your ideal on-the-day performance (covered in Chapter 15) ensures that you're relaxed and confident on exam day.

By rehearsing your recall before the exam (see Chapter 14), you know what information has been assimilated into your memory and what information is still floating around somewhere. When you know you can recall your study notes, you'll feel more confident going into the exam. That's a good thing, right?

Recall involves using memory techniques to remember information. Using your newly condensed, visually formatted study notes, you memorize and rehearse all your keywords by using methods that match how your brain is wired to think and learn — using one (or more) of the four primary learning styles, which I explain in Chapter 3:

- ✔ Visual
- ✔ Auditory (listening)
- ✔ Kinesthetic (feeling/doing)
- ✔ Analytical

In Chapter 14, I outline different recall techniques and show you how to develop a rehearsal timetable as exams draw near.

Rehearsing your performance involves visualization to mentally rehearse how you want to perform on the day (see Chapter 15). Your ideal scene, repeatedly rehearsed, will condition the response you want when you do the exam in reality. You have expanded your comfort zone ahead of time and with your anxiety at a minimum, you can maximize your exam performance.

Chapter 2

Meeting Your Amazing Brain

· ·

In This Chapter

▶ Understanding how your brain works and develops with learning

▶ Discovering some reasons why sometimes you just don't get it

▶ Making the most of some key learning principles

▶ Exploring the different types of brainwaves

▶ Maintaining and improving optimal brain functioning

· ·

*H*ave you ever bought software, installed it, and then not bothered to figure out how to use it to improve your machine's performance? If you've gone to the trouble of buying the software, you want it to work well — right? This analogy can be likened to your brain. You don't need to be a brain surgeon, but if you understand a little bit about how your brain works and know how to maintain its optimal functioning during exam time, you'll be in a much better position to discover more of your brain's capabilities.

In this chapter, I give you a brief overview of some of the relevant functions of the brain and how you can improve your brain-cell development.

You Don't Need to Be a Brain Surgeon

Recent brain research shows that the brain has an amazing adaptability to physiologically adjust to the learning demands you place on it. Called *neuroplasticity*, this simply means you can rewire your brain to think and learn anything. (I provide more background information on this amazing phenomenon in "Exploring neuroplasticity: Why the past doesn't equal the future" later in this chapter.)

You don't need an in-depth knowledge of all the different parts of your brain and how they function to use it properly. However, a basic understanding of how your brain works is useful to build confidence as you learn stuff through the year and revise for exams.

Understanding How Your Brain Functions

Your brain has three major parts (that's why it's called the *triune brain*) that evolved over time:

- The hindbrain consists of the brain stem (pons, medulla, cerebellum, midbrain, and diencephalon), which is connected to the spinal cord and controls your most basic instinctive drives and responses, such as breathing and heart rate. The brain stem also takes care of information from your senses and coordinates the instinctive movements of your body for your safety and survival.

  Interestingly, in states of extreme stress, your hindbrain becomes active, blocking access to higher parts of the brain. This is why it can be extremely hard to think rationally when you're highly emotional. You need strategies to reduce stress first, if you want to study and learn effectively — particularly if you suffer from exam anxiety.

- The midbrain is the smallest of the major brain parts and is in the brain stem. It relays specific information from the sense organs to the brain. Through and around this region is the limbic system, which includes the hippocampus, amygdalae, parts of the thalamus, and septum. The *limbic system* is regarded as the key player in how emotions, motivation, and long-term memory operate.

- The forebrain, or *cerebral cortex* (also called the *neocortex*), physically covers the midbrain and is the most evolved section of your brain. Your forebrain enables you to think and reason, set goals, and think abstractly, thereby setting you apart from other animals. Noted for its gray color, the forebrain controls the use of language and other responses received through the senses.

Figure 2-1 shows a cross-section of a human brain with the three distinct areas.

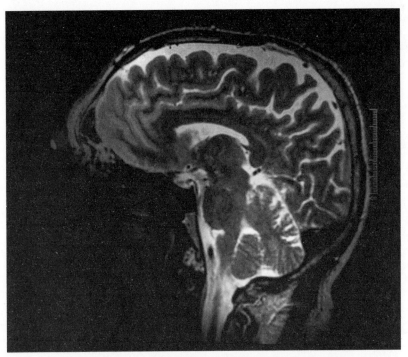

Figure 2-1: The human brain has distinct areas that perform different functions.

 Under the cerebral cortex (and part of the forebrain), lies the limbic system, made up of the amygdalae, hippocampus, basal ganglia, and septum. Together these are important for learning because it is currently believed that they regulate emotion, memory, and some aspects of movement.

The cortex contains billions of *neurons* (brain cells) that are connected to each other by tiny, tree-like branches called *axons* and *dendrites*. The connection point where two axons meet is called a *synapse*. You're born with approximately 100 billion neurons, and the number of connections increases between these neurons as your brain processes more information — that is, as you learn more. Interestingly, neurons make up only 7 percent of your brain cells. The larger number, some 76 percent of your brain cells, are glial cells called *astrocytes*.

TECHNICAL STUFF

Digging deeper into the forebrain

The forebrain has two structures — the telecephalon and diencephalons:

✔ The *telecephalon* shows the outer layer of the brain — the two hemispheres and the four lobes. The occipital lobe is for vision; the temporal lobe is for hearing and speech; the parietal lobe for sensory responses; and the frontal lobe for motor control and co-ordination. However, if serious damage happens to any parts of the brain, neuroplasticity research is now showing that the brain will draw on other regions to take up the demands that the damaged part is now unable to do.

✔ The *diencephalon* holds the thalamus and hypothalamus. It is believed that the thalamus helps transmit sensory information into and out of the forebrain. The hypothalamus monitors information coming in from the autonomic nervous system and controls bodily needs like hunger, thirst, and temperature. This is essential because it keeps your brain and the rest of your body supplied with its vital survival needs.

Astrocytes reside in large numbers, or domains, around the connection point (synapse), of your neurons. Exciting research in this area has brought in a new understanding about how neurons communicate, which has led to a new theory called the tripartite model, which I explain in the next section.

The Tripartite Model: How Brain Cells Develop During Learning

When you're learning something new, physiological changes occur in your brain. Your neurons (see Figure 2-2) sprout new branches and connect with other neurons to form neural pathways. Traditionally, scientists thought that the brain learns through the connection of one neuron to another at synapses. However, due to advances in brain-imaging technology, a third connection has become apparent, making a tripartite synapse.

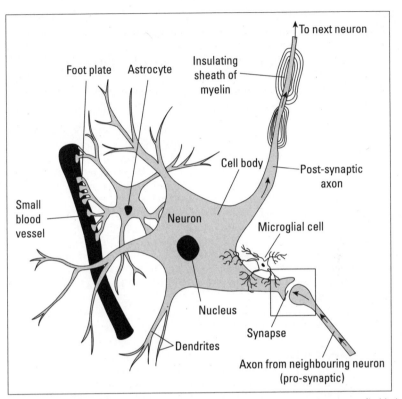

Figure 2-2: A brain cell (neuron) showing axon and dendrite branches. Astrocytes (behind the neuron) rest in groups, or domains, near the synapse.

 Many researchers currently say (and this is being developed as more studies are done) that, as neurons are communicating between each other through an electrochemical process, astrocytes are simultaneously tracking the chemical exchanges happening at the synapses. If a recurring neural pattern occurs, astrocytes map and automate the pattern so that the information no longer has to be consciously thought about.

All your habits and routines — the things you do without thinking — were constructed by the tripartite model of neural and astrocyte communication.

Do you remember learning your times tables when you were young? If you learned by rote (lots of repetition), your neurons responded by building neural pathways to that content, and because of the repetition, the recurring pattern enabled the process to be automated. Now you can rattle off 5 times 5 equals 25 and 5 times 6 equals 30 so easily you don't have to think about the mathematical calculations.

The same ability applies to learning more complex knowledge and physical abilities such as driving a car. You don't have to consciously pay attention to the range of tasks you accomplish when you drive a car — steer, accelerate, listen to music, notice your environment, talk to your passenger. Yet all of these tasks come flooding through your senses firing repeated neural patterns. Before long, astrocytes map the patterns, then automate the process so now you can drive in a free-flowing nonconscious way while thinking about something else. Only when something unpredictable happens, such as a cat running across the road in front of you, do you bring your attention out of this nonconscious driving state and back to your conscious attention.

Your brain is incredibly efficient. A mere seven percent of your brain cells are neurons and these respond to a huge amount of sensory input. To prevent you from experiencing neural sensory overload, astrocytes, which make up 76 percent of your brain cells, automate the activity. This frees up your neurons to consciously work on the next information you're taking in.

When you're confused while learning something new, it could simply mean that your neurons and astrocytes have not made enough connections yet. You don't have enough previously gathered knowledge for your brain to connect the new information into ideas that you can understand. Don't despair; persevere!

The way neurons and astrocytes communicate have two important learning implications:

✔ **Physiological:** You can improve the quality and number of synaptic connections in your brain simply by learning more about your world. Therefore, intelligence is not fixed but develops with the demands of ongoing learning. This applies not only to considering new knowledge and ideas, but also to learning new abilities and skills, such as playing a musical instrument or learning a new sport.

✔ **Psychological:** Even if your experience of exams has been less than optimal, the future can hold a new potential when you know how to improve the transmission between brain cells. Your confidence and self-esteem can increase because you know that the past doesn't control the future. You have the power to change the way your brain is wired by the way you study, practice, and rehearse the information. The stronger your brain cells integrate new information, the better your understanding and retention, and hopefully, the better your exam results! (I cover some key principles of learning and studying in the next section.)

How the human brain thinks, learns, and remembers is incredibly complex. The information in this chapter is a basic overview of the tripartite model based on some of the current literature. However, today's up-to-the-minute information is likely to be completely revised within the next few years as research methods improve. What this model does offer, however, is some useful information and key principles you can use as a student in your learning and exam preparation. If you're interested, keep a close watch on Google Scholar using the keywords **tripartite relationship between neurons and astrocytes**.

Making the Most of Your ASSETs: Some Key Principles for Learning

Your brain learns through sensory, emotional, and reflective-thinking processes that create memories. Researchers have identified some key principles that can help you improve your learning and studying skills.

Use the acronym ASSET to help you recall the five principles that can improve your learning and exam preparation. Write out this checklist and put it in your study space as a reminder to help you make the best use of your time:

✔ **Attention:** Learning requires your brain to respond to information coming through your senses. This sensory input is enormous in any given moment making it impossible for your brain to consciously notice it all at once. Your brain has an information selection process that blocks out sensory input you regard as not significant in that moment.

✔ **Senses:** Increasing the number of senses receiving information means increasing your neural and astrocyte activity. The quality and quantity of brain-cell communication means knowledge and understanding can pass more readily from short-term to long-term memory.

✔ **Solid effort:** The amount of conscious effort you put into understanding and retaining information helps determine how readily it is passed from short-term to long-term memory. Your ability to think about and reflect on knowledge builds new neural networks and strengthens existing networks as you integrate new information so that it becomes retained knowledge you can later access from memory.

✔ **Emotion:** If positive emotion — curiosity, anticipation, excitement, to name a few — is present during the experience when neural activity responds to any sensory input, this helps release more neural chemistry. The hippocampus (part of the limbic system), registers the increase in neural chemistry and upgrades the information to long-term memory more quickly.

✔ **Time sequence:** How often and how long sensory information engages neural activity plays a key role in how well you embed knowledge into your memory. Repetition is important and so is the amount of time between your repetitions. I discuss this factor in the section, "Minding Your Timing."

Paying attention

How often have you felt that information is going in one ear and out the other? You hear a teacher but don't listen to a single word; you read a page of a textbook but have no recollection of its content. There's a physiological reason for this occurrence and it involves how your brain receives information. Paying attention is the first of five principles that help you get that information to stick!

Understanding your brain's information selection process

Researchers believe that the brain has an information selection process that directs your attention and determines what you consciously notice. Because you are bombarded with sensory information, your brain has to choose what to notice and what to screen out. If you didn't filter input, you wouldn't be able to concentrate — you'd literally go insane from sensory overload.

So all sensory information has to be screened by your brain's information selection process, which decides what gets through to the cerebral cortex and, consequently, what grabs your conscious attention.

How does your brain decide what gets through? The answer, in general terms, is value. Only what's of value gets passed on to the cerebral cortex. Everything else, particularly if it is continuous and predictable, gets screened out. This is significant for students learning and taking exams because if you're tired, bored, uninterested, or dislike your teacher — basically if you see no value in what you're learning — your potential to learn the subject matter is significantly limited. Your brain shifts its attention to something more important — such as what you're going to have for lunch!

How can you get information into your head if your brain is screening lots of it out? The answer is twofold: through finding value and through relaxation.

- ✔ **Value:** You create value through a variety of methods. When information is novel, interesting, intriguing, engages your curiosity, or is suddenly different than what you expected, your conscious attention is switched on. (I talk more about these points in Chapter 4.)

- ✔ **Relaxation:** Similarly, relaxation can be used to slow your brainwaves, and slower brainwaves are conducive to learning. Research in this area shows some evidence that it can influence how your brain attends to sensory information. This is discussed further in the section, "Surfing the Waves of Your Brain."

You can easily see how your brain screens out some of what you are looking at by viewing some awareness exercises. Go to www.youtube.com and search for **awareness exercise**. In one clip, a group of basketball players is passing a ball around. Half the group is dressed in white, the other half in black. You're asked to count the number of passes the white group makes to each other. While your attention is focused on this group, something else happens. And incredibly, if you're like most people who watch the clip, you don't see it. Your attention is so focused on counting the basketball throws (the value) that the anomalous event gets screened out because the brain can only consciously attend to one thing at a time. Try doing this YouTube awareness exercise and see for yourself.

Finding value

If you didn't do well learning calculus at school, how come you learned history well, or learned to play a musical instrument, or to surf? Perhaps you just didn't care about calculus — couldn't see the point in it. If this is the case, your brain's information selection process prevented information from passing through to the cerebral cortex — your thinking brain — to be processed and consolidated into memory. However, if you find a way to make a subject valuable — that is, regard it with a sense of interest, intrigue, or curiosity — learning it becomes easier.

Exploring your attitudes to learning

Has anyone ever told you that you had a bad attitude? What is an attitude, anyway? I think of an *attitude* as an emotional response to an outside stimulus. In other words, a positive attitude is an emotional leaning toward something — you like it and want to experience more of it. A negative attitude causes you to lean away from a subject. If you have a negative attitude toward something you're learning, your attention becomes focused on something else and the information you could be learning is likely to be screened out.

Your attitudes can determine what value you place on learning, and your attention is driven by value. When you start to identify the attitudes and beliefs holding you back, you can begin to turn them around. To begin exploring your negative attitudes, try these steps:

1. **Identify an academic topic that's causing you difficulties and note the problem.**

   What specifically is the problem — your perceived ability, the difficulty of the content, or a challenging teacher? Write your answers down.

2. **Consider your reason or purpose for learning this material.**

   Do you have a big enough reason? What's motivating you? For example, perhaps you want to get a better-paying job?

3. **Ask yourself what beliefs could be holding you back, and write them down.**

The point in following these steps is that they help you identify a problem topic, assess its value (do you really care if it's a problem?), and expose attitudes or beliefs that may be blocking your progress. In Chapter 4, I explain how to condition helpful attitudes and beliefs through affirmation and visualization techniques so that you can move on.

When I was learning French in high school, I saw no value in it. Consequently, I found the subject difficult and eventually failed my French exam. In hindsight, I could have found value in learning French if I had thought of a personal goal. My goal could have been: Speaking French would help me impress the girls!

Setting a goal creates value, and value gets your attention focused on what's important. Find a purpose in what you're learning, no matter how small, and watch how your brain switches on. Attention, concentration, problem solving, and creativity can all be enhanced when you know what's of value. After you bring limiting attitudes into conscious awareness and create a goal that inspires interest, you are likely to reduce the difficulty you have with learning.

If you're experiencing difficulties and can't work on limiting attitudes or beliefs by yourself, consider seeking professional guidance. Techniques include hypnotherapy, which is becoming increasingly recognized as a helpful tool in improving learning and retention. (For more information on hypnotherapy, see Chapter 5.) You can also get professional exam-prep coaching online through my website at www.passingexams.co.nz.

Getting sensible

Involving a number of senses as you learn is the second principle to help improve learning. Chapter 3 talks about learning styles, or preferences in how your brain receives, processes, and communicates information.

It is generally accepted that the more senses used in the learning experience, the stronger and more complex the neural networks that develop. This improves the retention of sensory input, consolidating information from your short-term memory to your long-term memory.

A student I know recently commented that he finds learning by reading textbooks difficult. He had an important human anatomy exam for his sports and recreation degree coming up and his instructor wanted him to do a lot of reading. He chose another way. Instead of simply receiving sensory information by reading, he watched an educational video on YouTube in which an instructor taught the same content. My student friend was seeing, hearing, and experiencing the content through multiple senses. He remarked how much easier it was to learn all the technical terms and how much more interesting the learning process was! Consequently, he did well in the exam.

Using multiple senses to receive information is called *multimodal learning*. Learning is further enhanced when a solid effort is applied. This brings me to the third principle for rapid learning — effort.

Making a solid effort

The third principle using the tripartite model is the effort you apply to help improve your learning. As you reflect upon, question, and repeatedly review the content or activity you're learning, brain-cell networks are furiously building and strengthening. In turn, the knowledge you're creating gains stronger understanding, retention, and recall.

Educational consultant Mark Treadwell suggests that the learning process is initiated by a prompt that stimulates an emotion that in turn causes you to ask questions, which makes you curious. Applying effort by constantly reflecting, reviewing, and reiterating information helps build a knowledge base. This knowledge can form ideas that, if applied to a number of contexts, can form a conceptual understanding. With further reflection, different combinations of knowledge, ideas, and concepts can form a conceptual framework that allows the learner to predict new possibilities for other contexts. This is where creative and innovative ideas come from and what Mark and his colleagues believe will be the primary purpose for education in the 21st century. For more information about Mark Treadwell's educational paradigm shift work, please visit www.marktreadwell.com.

Engaging your emotions

The fourth principle listed in the ASSET acronym is emotion. A lot of research has been conducted into the link between emotion and memory, and still more is needed to really understand how they work together. Basically, researchers suggest that experiences that cause heightened emotion (as opposed to neutral emotions) seem to be remembered more easily. For example, can you recall your favorite holiday experience? Your long-term memory recalls it easily, right? It's believed that parts of the emotional center of your brain, the *limbic system*, interact with neural and astrocyte communication by releasing more hormones into the synapses during the formation of emotional memories.

Now try to remember a learning experience, perhaps with a favorite teacher. Do you recognize any emotion associated with it? Did the memory come back easily or not? If the association had a neutral emotional response associated with it, the likelihood that you'll be able to recall is low. However, if you associate emotions such as curiosity, surprise, excitement, or anticipation with a lesson, you're more likely to recall it.

The more positive the emotion you associate with your learning and the more emotion you can bring to preparing for exams, the more likely you are to retain and recall the information.

On the other hand, stress and its attendant negative emotions have the opposite effect. When you're feeling stressed, the brain's natural response is to release adrenaline as a stress hormone into neural networks and throughout your body. This can inhibit learning and memory retention. The good news is that you can quickly reduce excess adrenaline in your body/mind by a burst of physical activity.

For more information on techniques to help improve your memory, see Chapter 11.

Minding your timing

The fifth and final principle you can use to improve learning relates to how often and how long you review information. When playing a piano, if the individual notes are played with too long an interval between them, they produce no music. And so it is with your brain. If you leave too long a gap between your initial exposure to new information and your review of it, your memory retention is significantly reduced.

Memory studies suggest that retention is dramatically improved if you review what you initially learned within 24 hours. Your retention is further improved if you do a second review within a week and a third within a month. Every time you study the information, particularly in the first 24 hours, you are engaging and strengthening the brain-cell communication, and consequently helping to consolidate knowledge from short-term to long-term memory. This is discussed further in Chapter 11.

Surfing the Waves of Your Brain

Information coming through your senses — what you see, hear, touch, taste, and smell — passes through your brain cells by an electrochemical process. The movement of this energy creates brainwaves.

Exploring brain frequencies

Brainwaves function with five main frequencies of electrical energy measured in hertz (Hz), which can be measured with an electroencephalogram (EEG machine):

- **Beta waves** (13 to 30 Hz) are used in a normal, fully-awake state. All your senses are operating at this frequency, and the beta waves also direct your short-term memory while you're attending to daily activities.

  Interestingly, much of the modern world's technology operates at high beta levels. Your brain has a tendency to harmonize or synchronize with its external environment. However, being in a high-beta state for a prolonged period causes tension in your body. That's why when you remove yourself from technology and enter more natural surroundings — say, going for a barefoot walk in the park or along the beach — you begin to relax.

- **Alpha waves** (8 to 12 Hz) are generated when you're in a relaxed yet alert state, being aware of your outside surroundings. This is the ideal state for learning. Interestingly, young children operate more naturally from alpha state, which may explain why they're generally more easily able to absorb information than adults.

- **Theta waves** (4 to 7 Hz) emerge when you're deeply relaxed. Theta state can be reached through meditation or deep daydreaming and is beneficial for enhancing your creativity and problem-solving abilities. Long-term memory is easily accessed in theta state, so hypnotists use it in therapy.

- **Delta waves** (0.5 to 3 Hz) are the slowest waves and usually occur when you're sleeping. In this state, the automatic functions of the brain keep your life-support systems operating.

✔ **Gamma waves** (26 to 70 Hz, but often around the 40 Hz range) are associated with higher reasoning faculties that engage a number of different cognitive processes simultaneously. Gamma waves seem to be related to perception and consciousness because they disappear when you're under general anesthetic.

Training your brainwaves

Your brainwaves are highly flexible, and you can deliberately manipulate them for different purposes, such as enhanced learning and creative thinking, as well as relaxation and improved sleep. Accessing different types of brainwaves, called _brain entrainment_, has useful benefits for personal and professional development, one of which includes releasing learning potential.

You can cause your brainwaves to slow down and become more receptive to learning by relaxing your body through breathing and relaxation exercises or meditation techniques.

You can also use technology to help you train your brain to harmonize to beats and rhythms that oscillate in the alpha and theta ranges. Brain entrainment soundtracks help you to dip into deep levels of relaxation, releasing stress and calming your mind.

You can find brain entrainment software and audio products, such as soundtracks and CDs, on the Internet. Check out the Centerpointe Institute at www.centerpointe.com or type **brain entrainment** into your favorite search engine. You can also download free alpha-inducing relaxation music from my homepage at www.passingexams.co.nz.

Exploring neuroplasticity: Why the past doesn't equal the future

Only a few short decades ago, scientists believed that many areas of the brain, after they finished developing, remained unchanged for the rest of your life. However, one of the most amazing discoveries about the brain in recent years is how adaptable it is to environmental change. This adaptability is called _neuroplasticity_. Scientists discovered that, through neuroplastic treatments, people with difficulties, including physical problems caused by brain injury, learning problems, and even emotional problems, can essentially rewire their brains to address the problem.

Neural networks adjacent to damaged areas would take over for nonfunctioning gray matter, thereby strengthening weak existing networks. Certain environmental and mental stimulation actually altered thinking, learning, and behavior, and helped people to return to more normal functioning.

What does this mean for students? For one thing, it means that your past doesn't necessarily equal your future. Even if you've had problems mastering reading or writing or spelling — or any subject — you can improve in these areas because of your brain's ability to adapt to the demands you place on it.

Neuroplasticity may also explain why you're good at some subjects and poor in others. Over time your brain wires itself into certain types of thinking and learning processes that become habitual. You may be good at thinking logically and analytically for science, but when it comes to creative writing for English, you're challenged because your brain is simply not wired to think about language as it is to think about science. Current thinking suggests that this may be due more to your interest and attitudes towards the subjects and the amount of practice you did or didn't do! (For more information on this topic, check out learning styles in the next chapter.)

One common understanding people generally hold about the brain is that either your left or right brain is dominant. Previously, experts believed that the left hemisphere allowed more logical/analytical thinking, whereas the right hemisphere was creative, artistic, and musical. Nowadays, experts know that this is not the case.

Due to recently gained knowledge of neuroplasticity, some researchers now believe that logical and creative thinking can occur in different regions all over the brain and are not related to one side of the brain or the other. I guess you can dispel the myth that if you are good at math and science, you can't also be good at creative pursuits.

To discover some interesting views about this topic, go to www.YouTube.com and search **neuroplasticity**. Be sure to watch videos featuring Norman Doidge and Barbara Arrowsmith-Young.

Because of your brain's amazing ability to adapt and rewire itself, you can learn to improve your thinking, learning, and behavior by challenging your brain in different ways.

Neuroplasticity operates in both the realm of the physical and of the mind — both analog and digital, as it were! Researchers are using computer software and visual imagery to simulate environments that foster neuroplasticity in the brain. I discuss the idea of using mental rehearsal or visualization to strengthen brain-cell communication, memory, and ability in Chapter 4.

Getting Yourself Firing on All Levels: Brain Maintenance

How well do you look after the vehicle you use to get you where you want to go? Do you actively make sure it's well maintained? Ongoing maintenance ensures that your bike, car, or scooter is running well and gives you confidence that you can reliably get from place to place. Your brain requires ongoing maintenance too. If you feed it, water it, and take it for a walk regularly, it can provide you with energy, motivation, concentration, and focus — great for your thinking processes during exam time. So how can you keep your brain in good working gear? The information in the next sections tells you.

Maintaining optimum health

Have you ever noticed that on cold days, when all the doors and windows of a classroom are shut and everyone is breathing each other's air, you feel like yawning before long? Not having enough oxygen causes drowsiness.

If you don't eat breakfast, by mid-morning your tummy is probably rumbling, and a hungry tummy reduces the energy-giving nutrients to your brain. Likewise with water — dehydration is a major cause of lapses in concentration. Feel your lips: If they're dry right now, chances are you're slightly dehydrated.

Brain-food supplements

Although scientists disagree about their effectiveness, some supplements are considered great for your brain. These include omega 3 and 6 oils (fish oil capsules); lecithin, a vitamin B complex with extra iron; and the herb gingko. Dark chocolate and peppermint are also considered good for your brain.

You can buy all these products at a supermarket. You can ask a naturopath or someone at a local health food shop for more specific advice. Tell them you're studying for exams and ask what they recommend.

Your brain works through electrochemical processes. A lack of oxygen, nutrients, or water reduces its efficiency. Your brain consumes 20 percent of the air you breathe, 40 percent of all nutrients in your bloodstream, and 30 percent of the water you consume. Your blood carries the energy-giving nutrients and oxygen to your brain, and blood is 83 percent water!

To ensure optimal health for brain efficiency, pay attention to these health factors:

- ✔ **Exercise:** With everything going on in your life, it's easy to get tired, stressed, or anxious, especially when exams are looming and you have a mountain of studying to climb. Regular exercise is a great way to reoxygenate your blood. Walking, running, dancing — doing any physical exercise for at least 20 minutes several times a week — helps keep your brain effective and alert.

- ✔ **Oxygen:** Your brain needs plenty of oxygen in order to keep functioning effectively. In fact, almost one-quarter of your oxygen intake goes to supply your brain. If you're studying hunched over a desk or sitting at a computer for hours on end, your breathing is probably shallow, and you're likely to begin feeling drowsy.

To stop yourself feeling drowsy, sit up straight and do some deep breathing down into your stomach. Do this without expanding your chest. Make sure you get the residual air out of your lungs. A good way to do this is to breathe in through the nose for a count of 4, hold it for a count of 16, and then breathe out through your mouth while you count to 8. This re-oxygenates your brain and makes you more alert. Repeat this process ten times, and then return to your study.

Another breathing exercise is to breathe in through your nose, exhale through your nose, then hold your breath for as long as is comfortable without much air in your lungs. Then breathe normally again and notice how you feel. This technique has been used with people who suffer from asthma and need to get more oxygen into their blood. Helpful for students too!

✔ **Nutrition:** Good nutrition and good learning go hand in hand. The efficiency of the brain's electrochemical neural activity is dependent on the quality of its neurotransmitters. Neurotransmitters are made from amino acids, which are derived from proteins in your diet. Vitamins and minerals in foods help convert amino acids into neurotransmitters.

Your brain gets its energy from glucose (sugar) contained in carbohydrates. Fruits, grains, and vegetables are rich in carbohydrates, which dissolve through digestion into glucose. Ensuring that your glucose levels remain stable is important to avoid experiencing lethargy or mental confusion. A lack of energy can easily be mistaken by your teacher for disinterest or apathy. If you experience this, try to eat something substantial as soon as possible.

Fats are important too. More than half of the brain is composed of fat. Each neuron has a covering of fat called a *myelin sheath*, which aids the speed of the nerve impulse. Fat also regulates memory and mood. Thinking processes can be slowed when there's not enough fat in the diet, but, as you probably already know, too much fat is detrimental as well.

✔ **Hydration:** Although you draw your energy from food, effective brain functioning comes from drinking plenty of water. Your brain dehydrates quickly. Even without consciously feeling thirsty, you can lose concentration and motivation because your brain is not getting the oxygen and nutrition from your blood — and remember, blood is 83 percent water!

When studying, always keep a water bottle handy and try to drink up to two liters a day. If you can't drink that much, supplement your water intake with plenty of fruits and vegetables, which are high in water content. Stay away from high-sugar energy drinks.

Getting physical

Brain gym exercises help you prime your brain for learning by relaxing your body and strengthening your mind. For example, brain gym exercises created by United States brain researchers Dr. Paul Dennison and his wife Gail involve simple body movements that also stimulate the brain. These movements (also called *Educational Kinesiology*) get both sides of your brain synchronized and help slow down your brainwaves.

The three main types of brain gym movements cover:

- Any cross-over movements of the arms or legs that synchronize the left and right hemispheres of the brain, such as walking, dancing, and juggling. Try lifting your knee up to touch your opposite elbow, and then do the same on the other side. Repeat this exercise six times.

- Any lengthening and stretching movements that release tension and aid relaxation, such as those described in Chapters 5 and 6.

- Energizing movements that help increase concentration, such as opening your eyes wide and moving your eyeballs from side to side and up and down while breathing deeply.

For best results, do these brain gym exercises until you feel ready to proceed with your work. And remember that your brain also needs food, water, and air.

PATRICK SAYS

In my high school exam-preparation seminars, I offer students an energizing eye-movement technique that was part of an experiment I read about in a local newspaper. In a nutshell, two groups of students were given a test, but one group was given an eye-movement exercise prior to the test whereas the other group wasn't. When the test results were analyzed, the group who'd done the exercise performed 15 percent better recall on average than those who didn't do the eye-movement exercise. The exercise is really simple: Simply open your eyes wide and move them from left to right for 60 seconds. Try it and watch your friends laugh at you. But hey, if it works, use it, right?

Juggling with academic intent

One of the most fun ways you can strengthen your *corpus callosum*, or the bridge between your brain hemispheres, and engage more whole brain activity is to juggle.

When you juggle, the left side of your brain operates the right side of your body and vice versa. This means that as you pass balls between your hands, your brain is doing some complex neural development between hemispheres until it's wired in to allow you to do the activity automatically, without consciously thinking about it. This is what astrocytes are believed to do.

Progressing through the levels of learning

Getting to the point of automated mastery of a subject or skill involves four levels of learning, as shown in Figure 2-3.

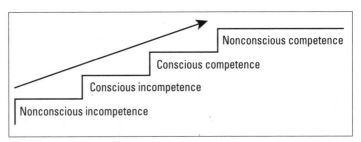

Figure 2-3: The four levels of learning. Confusion and frustration often occur in the two lower levels, at which point many people give up. Perseverance is the key to success.

When you're learning something new, you begin at the first level: *Nonconscious incompetence*, which means you're not good at something and you don't really realize this fact. The second level is *conscious incompetence*, in which you wake up to the fact that you're incompetent.

At these lower levels, your brain is still trying to make the neural connections and confusion and frustration often occur. When learning to juggle, for example, you frequently drop the balls at these stages, and it's very easy to give up and say, "I just can't juggle." The same process applies to learning anything new — mathematics, science, accounting, whatever. How often have you given up because you felt confused?

Your brain takes a little time to form neural networks. But by persevering, you reach the third level of learning: *conscious competence*, in which you start to get good at it. In time, with practice, you reach the fourth level: *nonconscious competence*. This means you're wired in to perform the thinking and behavior without consciously thinking. It's gone into free-flow mode.

Confusion is a natural part of the learning process. Confusion is good! During the learning process, you're likely to feel frustrated and confused at first as your brain works at wiring in a new way of thinking. Don't despair; persevere!

Teaching yourself to juggle

In my seminars, I often teach students how to juggle, and they're surprised at how easy it can be when they understand how their brain and thinking work to achieve the task. You can do the same by following these four steps:

1. **Prepare.**

   Tell yourself what your purpose or intent is for doing this task. What is your why? After clarifying your purpose, relax. Breathe deeply and allow your body to relax.

   To help your body and mind relax, use affirmation statements such as, "I can do this. I can learn to juggle." Try to see (and feel) yourself juggling in your mind's eye.

2. **Hold one ball in your right hand and two balls in your left. With your left hand release the front ball (of the two) and throw it across to catch it with your right hand. Then throw it back to the left hand. Repeat this sequence until it's wired in.**

3. **When you can do Step 2 without consciously thinking about it, turn your attention to releasing the single ball in your right hand. Ensure that the first of the left-hand balls comes over and think only of releasing the right-hand ball to catch it in your left.**

   Practice this movement until it's so smooth you don't need to think about your hand movements consciously.

4. **When you have two of the three balls passing between your hands easily, place all your attention on releasing that third ball as the second comes over. Aim to release the third ball to be caught in your right hand.**

   This step completes the ball-throwing sequence. With a little more practice, you'll find that you can repeat it over and over.

Congratulations! You used the four stages of learning to juggle three balls!

Chapter 3

Discovering How to Learn

. . . .

In This Chapter

▶ Setting up your ideal study environment

▶ Figuring out your best times for learning

▶ Discovering your preferred learning styles

▶ Exploring more thinking and learning styles

▶ Motivating yourself to learn

▶ Factoring in time to study

. . . .

*Y*ou may have heard statistics stating that the amount of information in the world today is doubling every two years. This means that what you learn in your first year at school will be outdated in your third year. More and more people will work in a number of different jobs before they retire. And advances in technology will require knowledge that hasn't been invented yet. The world is changing — and changing fast!

In order to keep pace with these changes and maintain your employability into the future, you need to know about the different ways that you absorb information so that you can adapt to the changes and manage your time more efficiently. If you can't learn quickly, you may be holding yourself back.

This chapter offers ways to build on how you learn best. I look at physical learning states to help you identify the type of study space you need to learn effectively. Then I explore learning styles to help you uncover the preferences your brain has developed for how it processes and communicates information. Motivation and managing your time are also key aspects to learning well. In this chapter you discover how to improve both areas to enhance your exam preparation.

Organizing Your Ideal Study Environment

One of the great things about human beings is their diversity. Everyone is individual and unique. As such, when it comes to studying for exams, everyone has their own personal strategy, developed over time from educational experiences in the past. Yet all individuals tend to use habitual ways of learning that were developed at school as a child, and often revert to familiar learning styles even if they're not the best ways for them to learn.

Most students who perform well at academic studies use learning states and styles that fit the way the school or university achieves things. Education is produced for the masses, with time and financial parameters influencing the quality and quantity of learning that each individual student is subjected to.

Students who don't fit this mass-produced generic approach and who fall by the wayside may not know how to work within the system or aren't aware of their ideal learning states and styles. This certainly doesn't mean they can't learn (although many people grow up believing they can't). Keep in mind that some of the world's greatest thinkers and achievers left school at an early age because they couldn't adapt to the dominant teaching style.

People can adopt different strategies to learn and study. Use the factors that influence learning in the following list to help you identify your own current strategies. Make a note of the conditions that best suit you.

- **Location:** Do you think you learn best in a classroom setting, in a library, at a friend's place, outdoors, or in your bedroom at home?

- **Room:** Do you prefer your study area to be tidy and well organized, or do you feel more comfortable amid clutter?

- **Lighting:** Do you prefer a dimly lit room with a table lamp or do you like a well-lit room with overhead lighting?

- **Temperature:** Does this make a difference to you? What temperature do you usually prefer? Your location and the time of year when exams fall may help determine how cool or warm you like your space.

- ✔ **Sound:** Do you prefer studying in silence, or with soft music, popular music, a ticking clock, the radio going, background chatter, or traffic noise?

- ✔ **Smell:** Do you burn incense or essential oils when studying? Inhaling certain smells, such as peppermint, is believed to enhance mental clarity.

- ✔ **Posture:** Do you like to sit on a chair at a desk, lie down on a bed, or move about? How you sit or lie makes a difference to how you feel over extended periods of concentration.

- ✔ **Food and drink:** What do you drink and eat while studying for exams? Consuming plenty of water and energy snacks allows you to maintain mental clarity and focus.

- ✔ **Time management:** How easily can you stick to a study schedule? Do you like to be super-organized or do you prefer just to cruise?

Essentially, you're looking to identify ways to create learning states that are comfortable, relaxed, organized, and free from distractions. When you know what states suit you, you can prepare your ideal learning environment, which in turn enhances your ability to prepare for and ultimately pass your exams.

Setting up your study space

Where you study matters because the environment you study in either helps or hinders your ability to think, learn, and review. Studying on the kitchen table may give you space, but if you're constantly distracted by movement in the kitchen, especially around meal times, you'll lose your train of thought.

Everything in your environment can affect your concentration, so it's important that you create a space that supports your learning and study efforts and doesn't disrupt you.

If you're unable to set up a room for yourself, designate an area of a room with a large table and comfortable straight-backed chair. This is your study space, so proclaim it to the household and be sure it's not taken over by other people's stuff.

Use these tips when setting up your ideal study space:

✔ If you can't get your own room, use a wall divider to separate your space from the rest of the room.

✔ Ensure that the chair you sit in is comfortable and provides good back support, so that you're not hunched over for hours on end.

✔ Make sure that you have plenty of drawers and shelves so that you have adequate storage, and everything you need is within reach. You don't want to become distracted trying to find stuff.

✔ Place inspiring comments, pictures, or visual representations of your goals on the walls around your space. These help keep you motivated and focused on the bigger picture to account for all that hard work you're doing.

✔ Install good lighting — a desk lamp or good overhead light. Poor lighting causes eyestrain, which reduces concentration and, in turn, motivation.

✔ Ensure that you have good air. Make sure you're close to a window you can open so that from time to time you can breathe deeply to keep oxygenating your blood. Burning essential oils, such as peppermint, black pepper, and basil, also help to enhance mental clarity. Bring a few plants into your study space to help purify the air.

✔ Set the mood. Music is good as long as it doesn't distract you. Use soft classical baroque music or high-tech music to help you relax and induce the alpha brainwaves most conducive to studying. (I explain how to alter your brainwaves in Chapter 2.) Familiar music is okay as long as the lyrics don't distract your conscious mind and break your concentration.

Eliminating distractions

One of the most common problems students face when preparing for exams is their inability to focus well during review sessions because of distractions. To help diminish distractions of all types and maintain focus, use these tips:

✔ **Reduce outside distractions.** If you set up a good working environment that's removed from the other areas of the house and is comfortable and well organized (as I describe in the preceding section), then you should be free from most external distractions.

✔ **Reduce your internal distractions.** If you're prepared for study, comfortably fed and watered, exercised and alert, and you're free from mental anxieties, such as relationship problems or money worries, then you should be internally ready and tuned for the work at hand.

A good way to deal with internal distractions, such as worrying, is to shelve the problem by making a contract with yourself not to think about the issue until after your study session. This may be impossible if your *limbic system* (the region of your brain that deals with emotions) is working overtime. Any highly emotional state is difficult to control with rational thought, so you just have to do the best you can to get through.

One quick strategy to deal with strong emotions is to actually delve into them and feel them intensely. The adage — what you resist persists — holds true. Trying to stop yourself from feeling unhelpful emotions may actually cause them to become stronger. Give yourself permission to feel them (when the time is appropriate) and let them pass through you and away.

✔ **Stay focused.** You'll lose concentration if you don't have clear reasons for putting yourself to this work. If you can set goals and intentions and find some value in what you're studying, generally you'll have no problem staying focused and keeping the concentration levels up. (In Chapter 4, I provide a lot more information on setting goals.)

Sometimes it's impossible to eliminate all the distractions from your study time, so be flexible. Organize those things you have power to control and let go of those things you aren't able to change. For example, you can't easily change your body's natural rhythms and alertness cycles when you start to lose concentration, but you can work around them by choosing good times to study (see the section "Knowing Your Best Times for Learning" later in this chapter).

Using a distraction scale

A *distraction scale* is a good way to pinpoint those things that interrupt your pattern of thought when you're trying to concentrate. You can then take steps to avoid them. Einstein used a distraction index when he was developing new ideas.

Imagine yourself preparing for exams. As you sit there trying to study, consider all the possible scenarios that could butt in and distract you from your work — a ticking clock, outside noises, people talking, your phone ringing. List each scenario on a piece of paper and beside each one draw a little distraction annoyance scale, a short line with evenly spaced numbers from 1 to 5:

>   1 = not annoying
>
>   2 = a little annoying
>
>   3 = annoying
>
>   4 = quite annoying
>
>   5 = really annoying

Now, add a mark on the scale to indicate the annoyance level that would cause you to become distracted.

Against each distraction scale number, think of a solution that could bring that annoyance level down the scale (say from 5 to 2) or off the scale altogether. For example, if your little brother barging into your room when you're studying warrants a 5 on your annoyance scale, one solution is to tell your brother not to come in when there's a sign on the door. Put a sign up saying something like: "Review in progress — please do not disturb." If that doesn't work, barricade yourself in!

Sometimes you won't be able to eliminate the distraction but, with a creative solution, you can at least reduce the annoyance level on your scale.

Some of your distractions are actually quite pleasurable. Stopping to get a snack or walking the dog, while being distractions, actually feed your brain's desire for pleasure. If you find yourself stopping your study every five minutes, use these pleasurable distractions as a reward. Give yourself a goal that after a set amount of studying — say, 30 to 50 minutes — you will reward yourself with a snack, or a walk — or both! Use the reward to motivate yourself to concentrate for longer periods of time.

Knowing Your Best Times for Learning

Everything in life has rhythms. The sun, the moon, the seasons, and ocean tides all work to a rhythm. So do human beings. You have daily, monthly, and yearly *circadian rhythms*, or body rhythms that influence your feeling of well-being and personal effectiveness. For example, do you consider yourself an early bird (a morning person) or a night owl (an evening person)? Do you find yourself naturally feeling sleepy between 2 p.m. and 4 p.m. in the afternoon and then tend to fell re-energized in the early evening?

Becoming more aware of your natural body rhythms helps you to determine your best times for learning. You can then plan to work when your mind is most awake, energized, and able to maintain concentration and focus.

One way to figure out your typical daily body rhythms is to draw a simple line graph highlighting how awake and energized you are during a typical day. Follow these steps:

1. **On a lined piece of paper draw the Y axis and name it "Alertness level." Draw a scale numbered 1 to 5, with 5 at the top in which 5 = highly alert, 4 = very alert, 3 = quite alert, 2 = barely alert, and 1 = not alert.**

2. **Name the X axis "Time of day," then draw a scale from left to right showing the hours of the day, starting with the time you wake up and ending with the time you typically go to bed.**

3. **Plot your alertness during the course of a standard day, then join the dots to produce a chart showing your normal body rhythms.**

The chart in Figure 3-1 shows my best times to study and take advantage of energizing body rhythms: From 10 a.m. to 1 p.m. and between 5 p.m. and 7 p.m. Working at other times is alright, of course, but my body may not be at its best energy levels.

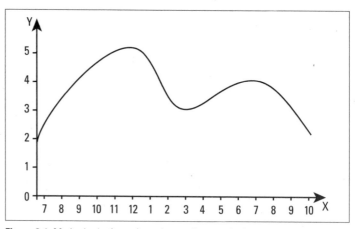

Figure 3-1: My body rhythms show that my best study times are late morning and early evening.

Discovering How You Learn Best

When learning new material, you use all your senses — sight, sound, touch, taste, and smell — but often your brain has already developed a preference for a particular method for receiving, processing, and communicating information. This is known as a *learning style*.

The following sections outline the four primary learning styles — visual, auditory, kinesthetic, and analytical. Although you may find you're dominant in one or two of these modes, the ideal is to develop your less dominant learning styles as well, so that you start using more of your brain-cell processes to meet the demands of learning.

 A number of researchers believe there isn't enough research to suggest that understanding your learning styles helps improve academic results. However, when I was studying, I found them useful to know about and used a lot of different approaches to studying. Consequently, I think you might find them interesting at least so that you can decide for yourself!

Seeing it: Visual learners

Visual learners learn best by seeing pictures in their mind's eye. They like to make lists, see charts, work with diagrams, and read things on the actual or virtual page.

The best method for visual learners to review information is to convert all linear notes to visual formats (using concept maps, such as those I talk about in Chapter 10), then rehearse their recall by verbally reciting what they see in their mind's eye.

Hearing it: Auditory (aural) learners

Auditory learners hear information in their minds. They learn best by attending lectures and listening to seminars or CDs and other audio recordings. They like to give verbal instructions and rehearse ideas by talking to themselves.

The best way for auditory learners to study is to arrange notes in visual format and convert them to audio recordings, then rehearse their recall by listening and verbally reciting the ideas aloud. Getting together with friends and batting ideas and information to and fro is also helpful.

Feeling it: Kinesthetic (physical) learners

Kinesthetic learners like to move about. They learn by feeling and doing through both physical, tactile feeling and emotional feelings. They're often sitting or lying comfortably and fidgeting with a pencil or pen.

The best way kinesthetic learners review information is by converting their notes to visual formats and rehearsing their recall by stating the information aloud while acting it out with great emotion. The more ideas they can convert to tactile feeling and movement (for example, writing notes and using cue cards), the better their recall.

Understanding it: Analytical (logical) learners

Analytical learners use logical, hypothetical reasoning to learn new information. They're the scientists, researchers, and computer programmers of the world. Their best study method is to convert their notes to visual format and rehearse their recall by verbally reciting the ideas in a logical way, as if they're teaching the ideas to their friends. Information has to be analytically understood before teaching can take place.

Developing your learning styles

After you identify the primary channels your brain prefers to use to receive and communicate information, it's easy to see why another channel may not be the best learning approach for you. For example, if you're primarily a kinesthetic learner and learn best through movement and feeling, you probably find it difficult to sit still at a desk and listen to a teacher or lecturer who's using primarily an auditory (speaking and listening) mode. Obviously, the trick is to develop all channels equally, so that you're not held back by a system that uses predominantly one means of communicating information. Combining a variety of learning styles may be helpful for more effective long-term learning.

I provide more information on developing learning styles throughout this book. The sidebar, 'Taking the online learning styles quiz' can also help. I also include a quick learning-styles quiz in Appendix C.

To discover other factors that influence learning styles, see the sidebar "Deciding if you're an activist, reflector, theorist, or pragmatist."

There's not enough research to reliably state that learning styles exist and that the study approaches that use them are any more effective than any other approach. However, it is generally believed that if you experience the knowledge you're aiming to learn through multiple senses (many learning styles), then this causes increased brain-cell communication and consequently better understanding and memory retention of that knowledge. So one suggestion for using learning styles is to not take your learning style results too seriously. Use them as a guide to explore many ways to review, retain, and recall information. Mix them up a bit!

Taking the online learning styles quiz

How does your brain primarily receive, process, and communicate information? Everyone learns differently, but when you discover your preferred learning styles and identify which styles you're weaker in, you can match your review methods to the way your brain is predominantly wired to think and learn.

One way to discover your learning styles is to take a learning styles quiz. On the home page of www. passingexams.co.nz is a link to a downloadable quiz. The quiz focuses on eight learning styles. As well as identifying four core learning-style strengths — visual (seeing), aural (listening), physical (doing), and logical (analytical) — the quiz indicates your preference for reading/writing, verbal, interpersonal (learning with people), and sequential thinking.

Answer the questions and chart your own results on a graph that looks like the one here. The further out from the center you score, the stronger that style.

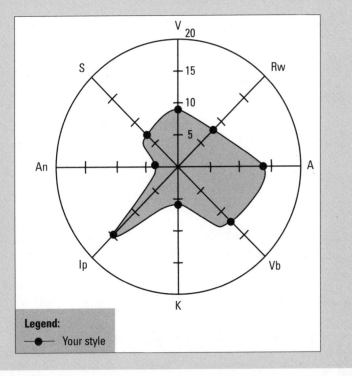

Legend:
— ● — Your style

(continued)

(continued)

After you take the quiz and see your strong and weak areas, you can choose a review format that matches the way your brain best processes information.

You can also practice those weaker styles to engage all of your brain.

For example, if you're not primarily an aural (listening) learner, you can strengthen that style by recording your notes to listen to or recite over and over.

Finding Out Whether You're a Linear or Circular Thinker

Understanding whether your thinking patterns are linear or circular (also called global) allows you to focus on how you learn best and tailor your approach to your study habits:

- ✔ A linear thinker has an overview of a topic and follows a logical sequence to understand it. Planning what needs to go in an essay from introduction to conclusion requires linear thinking.

  If you're the linear type, your preferred thinking style progresses in a logical flow — one step at a time. For example, planning and writing essays requires linear thinking — you need to organize your ideas in a logical sequence from introduction to conclusion. If you find it extremely difficult to plan and organize essay content, it could be that you think in a more circular fashion.

- ✔ A circular thinker needs an overview but comes to understand a topic from many different angles. This is a good synthesizing process in which many ideas can be integrated into one whole.

  This type of thinking is really useful as far as deciding what needs to go into an essay — less useful for deciding specifically where each piece best fits!

Different subjects require different thinking styles, and the difficulties you face with a particular subject could be related to the fact that you don't naturally think in the way the subject demands. Don't despair! Although you may be at an initial disadvantage, the concept of neuroplasticity (see Chapter 2) means that your brain can rewire itself to think in the new ways you demand of it.

Deciding whether you're an activist, reflector, theorist, or pragmatist

One way to understand your thinking and learning styles is to consider the theory of adult learning created by David Kolb and later adapted by Peter Honey and Alan Mumford to factor in personality traits. Ask yourself which one of these personalities relates most to you:

✔ **Activist:** These people are action oriented. The activist learns best through a variety of experiences, is open-minded, and is eager to try something new.

✔ **Reflector:** Learns by assimilating new information and taking time to reflect and discuss it with others. Likes to sleep on it.

✔ **Theorist:** Needs a clear and logical structure to learn new information. The theorist usually asks if something doesn't make sense and gathers information to clarify and formulate theories.

✔ **Pragmatist:** In order to learn best, these people need learning to hold relevant practical applications to their lives. The pragmatist enjoys learning new ideas from others and putting them into practice.

Although certain subjects require different ways of thinking, you can adapt your learning styles if you really want to. For example, if you see yourself as a strong pragmatist but need to theorize and reflect on a topic for an essay assignment, you may find that challenging. What you can do, however, is use your pragmatist skills to find the theorists and reflectors in your class and discover how they would approach the assignment. Then you can model your assignment from the ideas they offer you.

To discover your learning styles using this model, go to Peter Honey's website at www.peterhoney.com and take either the 40- or 80-item questionnaire. You have to pay Honey for the results though, so you'll need your credit card handy.

Another site that explores the concept of multi-intelligences developed by Howard Gardner (and offers a free, short questionnaire you can try) is the Birmingham Grid for Learning website at www.bgfl.org/bgfl/custom/resources_ftp/client_ftp/ks3/ict/ztiple_int/what.cfm. After you complete the questionnaire, you see which multi-intelligences are your strengths and the areas where you aren't so strong.

Alternatively, try asking someone who finds it easy (if you're a circular thinker, ask a linear thinker) for help. Don't forget that asking someone for help doesn't mean that you think she's more intelligent than you — her brain is just wired differently.

Getting Motivated to Study

There are a lot of theories about motivation within the academic paradigm. I explore some of the most common in the next sections.

Finding value in what you're learning

One of the prominent theories is that motivation is derived from two factors:

- ✔ The value you place on the task
- ✔ The expectation that you can achieve a good outcome

When exploring motivation in learning, consider the two types of value:

- ✔ **Implicit value:** You study for the sheer pleasure of learning the subject matter. You're motivated because you enjoy the subject, find it interesting, and feel curious to discover more.

- ✔ **Explicit value:** You're learning as a means to an end. Your motivation comes from achieving an external goal — for example, a grade or a qualification. You're not motivated so much by the joy of learning something new, but by the joy of achieving a goal.

Expecting to succeed is the flip side to the motivation coin. Research shows that people are more motivated if they believe they can achieve their goals. Self-belief creates a feeling of expectation — you know you can do it, and that knowing inspires motivation.

You can visually represent how motivated you feel by simply charting on a graph, as shown in Figure 3-2, plotting how much personal value you place and how confident you are that you can master the subject or pass the test.

The graph in Figure 3-2 shows that the person places high value (5) on the material. This may be either implicit or explicit value or some combination of both. However, the person's expectation of success is much lower, indicating that for some reason she doesn't believe she'll achieve the desired result. This indicates that a lack of motivation could result and that she needs to take some action in order to raise her expectancy level.

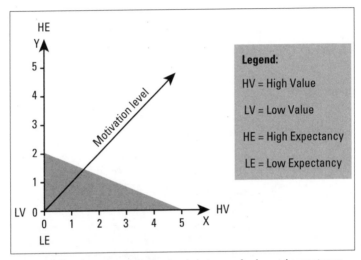

Figure 3-2: Charting your motivation levels in terms of value and expectancy for achievement: 5 = high, 1 = low.

In Chapter 4, I cover attitudes to improve your expectation for success in more detail. This includes looking at your self-efficacy beliefs — in other words, your own appraisal of your ability to achieve your goals. People with high self-efficacy set big goals because they believe they can make them happen, whereas those with low self-efficacy set easily achievable goals. Efficacy and expectation go hand in hand, because each relates to the beliefs you hold about your capabilities.

Beating procrastination

Other theories on how motivation affects learning explore how people creatively avoid tasks by engaging in procrastination or doing slovenly work.

You can overcome procrastination (and become motivated to learn) by

1. **Becoming clear on your goals.**

   Why are you studying and what are you aiming for? The more you value a topic, the more likely you are to naturally want to do it. For help with this, refer to "Finding value in what you're learning" earlier in this chapter.

2. **Identifying self-defeating problems.**

   Fear, anxiety, indecisiveness, and perfectionism can all be overcome through the right thinking. The first step is awareness. Make a list of possible limiting beliefs you may have about learning. One could be, "I hate writing essays." Later, when you have to write an essay assignment and are procrastinating, notice what inner self-talk is emerging.

   For more information on how to interrupt unhelpful thought patterns, see Chapter 4.

3. **Setting yourself small tasks to help build your confidence and self-efficacy.**

   Start small, then build to a higher standard. Really emphasize the positive. If you haven't achieved a standard you want, emphasize your effort over ability, then persevere.

Your past doesn't equal the future (refer to Chapter 2).

Try asking yourself the following questions and use the three-step strategy outlined in the preceding steps to reduce procrastination:

- ✔ **What's one thing I need to do today that I don't feel like doing but that will help me move towards my goal?**

- ✔ **What benefit will I get from doing this activity? Do I care?** Try to build the benefits — the value — in your mind.

- ✔ **Do I have a choice?** Think through the consequences of what will happen if you don't do it. If you can see more benefits, and you have the choice not to, you will feel more motivated.

Do the activity you came up with in answer to the first question.

Organize your time. Plot study dates on a weekly planner (see Appendix A for planning sheets you can copy). Set priorities and break large tasks into small ones.

One of the common procrastination challenges I hear from students is that they find it hard to even get started studying. My tip is to trick yourself: Tell yourself that you will study for just five minutes then take a break. This is usually enough to get you started, and generally 15 or 20 minutes pass before you even notice the time.

At the end of each day, make a list of the tasks you have to do the next day and rate them in order of importance. By prioritizing in this way, you make much better use of your time.

Try preplanning the day ahead before you go to sleep. As you lie in bed, imagine seeing yourself studying intently with great purpose. Then imagine feeling pleased about how much you accomplished in this day. You may be surprised at how this simple mental technique can help keep you in the flow as you move throughout your day.

Maintaining your concentration

In order to study effectively, you need good concentration. Can you sit and watch a full-length movie for hours and become totally absorbed? Can you perform an activity for large periods of time without thinking about what you're going to have for dinner? If you said yes to either question, perhaps your concentration is better than you think!

You want to be able to develop and maintain your concentration so that you can study for as long as 50 minutes at a time. There are no hard-and-fast rules on this however, so be happy with where you are now and work to improve it.

Your concentration can lapse for any number of reasons. Being aware of what those reasons are can help you get back on track:

- ✔ **Environment:** Dehydration, hunger, and a stuffy environment are the main reasons people start to lose concentration (refer to "Setting up your study space" earlier in this chapter). Don't forget to take quick breaks to stretch your body and breathe deeply.

- **Distractions:** External distractions are a major cause of broken concentration. Similarly, internal distractions, such as worrying, can prevent you from focusing. You can shelve your emotions during study times as I explain in "Eliminating distractions" and "Using a distraction scale" earlier in this chapter.

- **Personal value:** If you're interested in a topic, your concentration will remain high. If you can't see any value in your subject matter, try to create some. Perhaps you could look at the value you'd get from achieving a passing grade, despite not liking the topic.

Managing Your Review Time

Time management is another important area of preparation. This is where self-discipline comes in. How many distractions and little habits use up your valuable study time — calling a friend, preparing a snack, watching television? Make a list of distractions so that you become more aware of what they are when you study.

Also, identify the other areas of your life that take up a lot of your time. Are you over committed? Are there things that you can drop to give you more time for studying?

 Drawing up a timetable with all your academic deadlines can help you manage your time. A yearly or monthly planner is okay, but usually the scale is too large for working with regular deadlines. Better yet, create daily and weekly schedules using the templates I include in Appendix A. Using these planners helps you see exactly how much time you have to study and get assignments in on time.

Use time in your day that's otherwise unproductive. For example, laminate your notes and, while taking a shower, go over the details of a topic aloud. While traveling to class or work, listen to your recorded review notes on your chosen electronic device. Make use of as much spare time as possible. Twenty minutes a day spent this way is an hour and a half extra study time per week.

Another effective way to work when you're feeling under pressure to meet deadlines is to adopt a timeline strategy. This involves using a mental visualization technique that changes your inner perception of how much time you have left to achieve a particular goal.

Often, your brain perceives the situation as not having enough time to get everything done. It then sends stress chemicals to your body, which becomes tense. By changing your brain's perception of how much time you have left, your body can relax.

Try the following mental visualization technique.

1. **Close your eyes and take a deep breath or two.**

2. **Hold your arm out in front of you and point to your future.**

3. **Turn your palm up and visualize the work you still have to achieve and the deadline you want to meet.**

   For example, you may have an assignment due on Friday. In your mind's eye, you can see yourself actually handing in the assignment, knowing you have done the best you could. By placing this picture out in front of you, you're creating a timeline from where you are now to where you want to be on Friday.

4. **Now ask yourself, "How close does this deadline feel to me?"**

5. **Move your hand, palm facing you, slowly towards you until it feels like your palm is practically touching your face.**

   This is your physical representation of not having enough time. As you imagine the picture getting closer, your brain perceives a sense of urgency, which is what is making you feel stressed.

6. **Consciously move your hand back and visualize creating more distance between your present state and the future scene.**

   The scene will get smaller as it moves back, and you'll feel your body begin to relax. Although your physical time may not have changed, your brain's perception of the time you have left has changed. It thinks you have more time and will send signals to your body to relax a little more.

7. **Breathe deeply. Relax, and trust that you will meet the deadline.**

Chapter 4

Thinking Strategies for High Performance

· ·

In This Chapter

▶ Finding out how your mind absorbs and processes information

▶ Digging into your memory

▶ Exploring your memory of you

▶ Understanding how your self-talk governs your ability to learn

▶ Discovering how high-performing students think and behave

▶ Setting academic goals

▶ Using affirmations to condition yourself to reach goals

▶ Seeing yourself succeeding

· ·

*H*igh-achieving athletes often say that much of their success lies in being *in the zone* — a vague place where they're able to perform without consciously thinking about it. They operate on automatic; they've mentally and physically practiced so often that they can perform without consciously thinking about what they need to do (see Chapter 2 for more information on brain functions). Not having to consciously think about their movements allows them to maneuver quickly and easily.

Watch gymnasts at the Olympics, for example; they momentarily close their eyes just before their event. In their mind, they're visualizing the movements and using positive self-talk to engage their body and mind to get ready to act.

You can use these same strategies when you're preparing for exams and when you're sitting in that exam room; you imprint your memory to think like a high-achieving student, then let go and allow your performance ability to just go for it.

In this chapter, I give you a model of the mind that explains how you come to think the way you do. I explain how you can become stuck in the past and how to develop high-performing habits of thinking that can overcome some of the common challenges you face when preparing for your exams.

Understanding How Your Mind Works

The thing you call your mind is really the collective activity of your brain. Having a model that shows how your mind works is really helpful in improving any area of your life, because the quality and quantity of your thinking determines how your life goes. You can easily drift through life merely reacting to or avoiding situations, but there's another way of living: You can predetermine your experience by deliberately thinking positive, affirmative thoughts about your life before your life shows up!

The way you think directly influences how you perform in exams. For example, if you're in the workforce and haven't taken a test in many years, a really important career exam may cause you considerable anxiety. You may be thinking thoughts such as, "I hate exams," "It's been such a long time, I don't know if I can do it," or "I'm probably going to fail."

But do you know that you're a great prophet, foretelling your future with your negative thoughts? More often than not, *self-talk* (the way you speak in your mind) creates the unwanted response you most want to avoid: Failure! (For more on how self-talk affects your academic performance, see the section "Improving Your Self-Talk for Better Exam Results" later in this chapter.)

You can gain a greater feeling of control over the areas in your life you want to improve by focusing on what you want, not what you don't want. High-performing people actually do this thought process deliberately. Instead of basing your current thoughts on your sometimes unhelpful memory, you can consciously and deliberately think yourself into the future you want by using positive forethought. Start telling yourself, "I am doing this, and with some careful preparation, I will do well. I will pass this exam with ease."

Understanding how your mind works is important because you can then start to make it work more effectively for you. For example, think of the software that runs your computer. You need to read the instructions and play around with it to get it working properly. The same is true for you. Your mind is made up of two important aspects that determine not only how you behave, but also how you see your world. I cover both in the following sections.

Perceiving with your conscious mind

Your *conscious mind* deals with that part of your thinking that you're mostly aware of. Your conscious mind perceives and interprets your experiences through your senses in four stages: perception, association, evaluation, and decision-making.

For example, if your last chemistry exam was really difficult, when a new chemistry exam comes up, your brain makes an instant conscious association with the previous exam and predicts that the next exam will be difficult too. You may make the decision to prepare more thoroughly based on your past experience.

On the other hand, your friend, who took the same exam and believed it to be easy, may decide to spend less time preparing for the next test. His conscious mind's association and evaluation process led him to make a different decision. Same exam, very different perceptions.

So what's real or true for you is entirely because of your attitudes and beliefs that cause your thinking.

Delving into your nonconscious mind

Much of your brain activity (thoughts) operates beneath your conscious level of awareness. It is nonconscious. As you experience life, the thinking you have about all the experiences you've perceived and learned since birth form ideas about yourself and the world. These ideas are stored as a kind of autobiographical memory, often known as your nonconscious mind.

Using the analogy of an iceberg is a good way to illustrate how your mind works. In Figure 4-1, notice that only the tip of the iceberg is seen above the waterline. In other words, you're only consciously aware of a small part of your perception, reasoning, and behaviors. What really drives these are your nonconscious attitudes, habits, values, beliefs, and self-images stored in you memory.

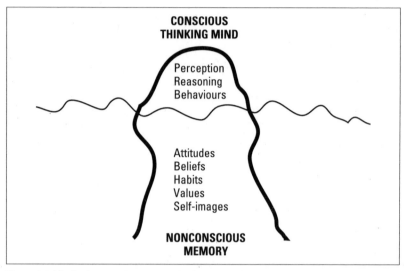

Figure 4-1: The iceberg analogy — much of your thinking power is below the surface.

Meeting Your Memory

Human memory has three functions:

- ✔ As your conscious thinking responds to sensory information, that information is encoded into your sensory memory.

- ✔ Information is received through your senses and processed from sensory memory to short-term memory then to long-term memory depending on the five principles outlined in Chapter 2.

- ✔ Processed information can be retrieved later when you want to remember it.

Memory is thought to have two main divisions:

✔ **Declarative memory** involves conscious recall in response to a cue. Also known as *explicit memory*, this type of memory is influenced by the *hippocampus*, a part of the limbic region of your brain (refer to Chapter 2).

Declarative memory is the knowledge you have encoded and retained about how you are and how the world is. Like your memory in general, declarative memory also comes in two forms:

• **Episodic memory** is knowledge you gained from the experiences you had in a particular time or place (a context). It is likened to the idea of autobiographical knowledge. "I am good at writing essays," is an episodic memory.

• **Semantic memory** is the conscious recollection of all the facts and general knowledge you've learned about the world that can be independent of any context. For example: "Essays need to be logically formatted by an introduction, a body, and a conclusion," is a semantic memory that provides understanding. The concept of essay writing can then be applied to any context — not just the context you learned it in.

✔ **Procedural memory** is memory you recall without a conscious cue. It is dependent on context. Known as *implicit learning*, procedural memory relates to motor skills such as knowing how to ride a bike or drive a car — things you can do without having to really think about them. High-performing athletes draw on well-developed procedural memory.

Conceptualizing Your Memory of You

By its nature, your memory is generally constant. Its job is to keep you being the same. If it didn't, your life would be utter chaos. Although your ability to recall knowledge over time may diminish, your episodic or autobiographical knowledge generally remains stable by default — you know who you are. You know your attitudes, beliefs, values, and habits of thinking — your memory of you. For example, "I am a quick learner," "I hate science," "I can't write good essays," and "I love history" are all beliefs you may have developed about yourself over time. This process of autobiographical learning is called *conditioning*.

Your conditioned beliefs are what drive your behavior, causing you to respond to situations from a belief level, not a potential level. You may be living well below your academic potential because of limiting or unhelpful beliefs about your ability or interest in learning.

Believing is seeing

Your brain deciphers your day-to-day experiences through the conditioning from the past. Your attitudes, beliefs, values, and habits of thought influence how you see the world.

One of the reasons you perceive situations differently from others is that your conditioning influences what you literally see and don't see. Sometimes you can look right at something and not see it. Take a look at the following statement:

> Worthy of further consideration is the fact that we find access to an abundance of information about the functions of the brain. This is the result of years of scientific research and study.

Now, as quickly as possible, count how many times the letter *f* appears in this statement. How many did you find? The answer is 11. If you missed an *f* or two, what you experienced is a sensory blocking out of visual information. Count them again, but this time pay attention to the word "of" in the statement. Did you find some more instances of the letter *f*?

One possible reason this happens relates to how you learned to read. If you learned *phonetically* — sounding out the words in your head — your brain probably interpreted "of" as "ov" so it didn't see the *f*. If you were taught to read visually, you would possibly see more. The point is, your conditioning — in this case, how you were taught to read — determined what you saw.

Another possibility is that your brain likes working efficiently and only selects enough information for you to get the meaning of the sentences. Because *of* is a small word, your brain skips over some of the *of*s because they add little to your understanding.

Ask some friends to read this statement and see how many *f*s they count.

Your beliefs about a subject determine how you perceive and experience it. This is an important point. If your beliefs influence your perceptions — for example, if you believe "history is boring" or "I don't understand accounting" — then you'll constantly block out information that doesn't match your beliefs. It simply doesn't get through!

You may also continually perceive and therefore behave in a way that reinforces your limiting belief — a self-fulfilling prophecy. So, until you can change your limiting belief about history or accounting, you will plateau at a particular standard, which seems impossible to improve on. Believing is seeing!

When I was a high school student, I used to believe I wasn't academically inclined. I never did particularly well at exams and didn't plan to go to university. I held these attitudes and beliefs for ten years before I finally decided to go back to school. As an adult student, I went to a university and within a short time started doing very well in higher education. I even won an award for excellence for being the top student in three social science subjects. This evidence began to transform my limiting beliefs. Before this experience, I didn't know how my mind worked. I didn't know that my memory was keeping me locked at my limited belief level, But more importantly, I didn't know I could change my beliefs! I now plan to earn a PhD one day.

Resisting change

Whenever you have a problem or difficulty or are out of your comfort zone and under stress (such as during an exam), your mind naturally works to fix the problem — to release the tension and help you return to a state of ease.

For example, if you think "I can't do calculus," as soon as you try to act beyond that belief and do better at calculus, your thinking, perception, and ultimately your behavior try to bring you back to what you know is true about you — back into your familiar truth.

Cognitive dissonance occurs when there's incongruity between what you perceive and what you believe. *Cognitive* means "thinking"; *dissonance* means "getting uptight" — or "a lack of consistency between beliefs." When there's a mismatch between what you see and what you know to be true, you experience an uneasy feeling and begin thinking thoughts that counter the perception.

Your mind tries to maintain how you predominantly see yourself (as a not-very-good student, for example) and causes you to think and behave in ways that are more familiar to the old you. For example, while you're observing yourself in an unfamiliar setting, attempting to study for an exam at the kitchen table, your conscious thinking is bouncing this experience off your nonconscious memory ("this isn't like me") and through dissonance, tries to pull you back to what's normal for you — watching television while munching donuts!

In an academic setting, you're often required to do activities that extend your current beliefs about your abilities. It may be a large assignment with a short deadline or an oral presentation in front of a large group. When you try to think or behave in a way that you believe is not like you, an uncomfortable dissonance occurs, forcing your mind to activate thinking and behavior that takes you back to how you know yourself to be.

Your mind may hold you back in various ways:

- ✔ **Engaging in negative or limiting self-talk:** Telling yourself, "I can't do this" or "I have a memory like a sieve" or "I'm going to fail."

- ✔ **Creating avoidance strategies:** Eating, going out instead of studying, watching television, playing on the computer.

- ✔ **Procrastinating:** Prioritizing study behind other activities that need to be done.

- ✔ **Ruining your concentration:** Letting your mind wander when you study and thinking of other things you would prefer to be doing.

- ✔ **Being distracted:** When you do study, you find yourself fidgeting or getting up a lot to get a snack, send a text message, or take the trash out.

- ✔ **Enhancing feelings of mental and physical anxiety:** When you're out of your comfort zone, such as going into an exam, your mind is giving you physical feedback, telling you this isn't familiar — the situation is not like you.

To start to correct these problems, you need to change your conditioning. You have to recondition your nonconscious memory on the inside so the idea that you're a hard worker who studies effortlessly and achieves excellent results in exams becomes the most dominant image in your mind.

Don't let your limiting beliefs hold you back from doing well academically. Believe me when I say that the past doesn't have to equal the future!

Improving Your Self-Talk for Better Exam Results

Your *self-image* (the beliefs you have about yourself) is maintained by the quality and quantity of your *self-talk* (how you speak in your mind). Some scientists believe that human beings think about 50,000 to 60,000 thoughts a day and that many of these thoughts are repetitive. The inner dialogue you have with yourself on a consistent basis imprints your memory to condition your beliefs. If said often enough, your memory accepts the self-talk as truth and makes sure you act in accordance with it. "I don't understand it, I must be dumb" is not going to improve your ability to learn. But, "I haven't learned this yet!" at least provides the opportunity to learn, even if it takes you longer than some people.

If you become aware of how you think of yourself in various academic situations, such as preparing for exams, you can start to identify the limiting self-talk that may prevent you from improving your exam performance. Look to identify the overall attitudes and feelings you hold about yourself in that situation, or in any situation, and make your self-talk positive and affirming.

When I work in high schools, I often hear from students who feel that a particular teacher causes them to do badly in class. Their self-talk might be: "I am failing English because my teacher is hopeless." This kind of self-talk takes the accountability away from those students. It leaves them with the feeling that if the teacher isn't doing a good job, they can't learn and ultimately can't do well on an exam for that class. I suggest that they need to decide how badly they want to pass the class. They need to set a goal and take responsibility for their own learning. One way they can do this is to change their attitude towards their teacher and watch to see if their teacher responds differently to them.

You can become more aware of limiting self-talk by wearing a rubber band on your wrist for several weeks. Whenever you catch yourself thinking a negative thought, flick the band to give yourself a sting. You can also help your friends. Whenever you hear your friends saying something limiting, you can flick their rubber bands to make them aware of slips.

If you don't want to use a rubber band, use a funny code word like *bananas*. This random word will help your brain interrupt the limiting pattern of thought. Figure 4-2 shows how self-talk impacts on your academic performance.

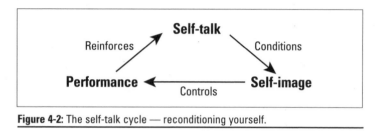

Figure 4-2: The self-talk cycle — reconditioning yourself.

Because your performance in any area of life (exams included) is influenced by how you see yourself — your self-image — make your self-talk affirming and positive.

The way you see yourself as a student is reflected in your academic performance. The first step to building your academic self-image — what your mind thinks of you as a student — is to start paying attention to your self-talk about learning and taking exams. Your self-talk conditions your self-image, and your self-image controls your performance. So you need to start to imagine yourself into higher levels of academic ability deliberately and make these the most dominant thoughts in your mind.

For a while you may have to live in two worlds simultaneously, observing current reality but holding your future vision as clearly as possible. In time, however, your future vision will become your current reality and you'll be thinking of an even bigger vision.

Exploring your self-efficacy

Self-efficacy is your appraisal of your ability to be able to create the life you want. It makes up some of the ideas you hold about yourself (your self-image) and determines whether you think you can or cannot achieve your goals.

Research shows a direct correlation between academic self-image and academic performance. Students with a strong academic self-image and high self-efficacy beliefs are more likely to perform better in class and in exams than those with lower self-efficacy beliefs.

Many students have subject-related self-efficacy beliefs — "I'm good at math" and "I'm not good at English" are two examples. So a student's academic self-efficacy can't be generalized across all subjects.

One way to build your self-efficacy is to make a list of all the successes you've had. Look outside academia at what you're good at — what you've been able to learn in the past. For example, how you learned to use a computer, text rapidly on your mobile phone, drive a car — anything you've become good at. Even a smaller version of your current academic goal is helpful. Then dwell on that feeling of achievement and see if you can bring it through to the current goal. If you can make connections between past successes that have developed self-efficacy, you can carry that through to new potential successes. In other words, if you learned to do A, you can learn to do B.

You can develop academic self-efficacy in stages by breaking your goals into smaller steps. As you achieve each little step, your self-efficacy strengthens. You start seeing evidence of your successes and, soon, you're telling yourself you *can* achieve this larger goal. Your self-efficacy beliefs become aligned with your goal and then positive feelings of expectation emerge. In a short time, your goal becomes a reality, and as the self-talk cycle suggests, you become encouraged to start thinking towards even greater successes.

Enhancing your self-esteem

Another aspect to your self-image is self-esteem. Your *self-esteem*, or the ideas you hold about what you feel worthy of receiving, is an estimate of your self-worth. They can take the form of standards or expectations, and they play a key role in your learning success. For example, if your self-esteem about learning is low, you won't feel confident or self-assured in learning new material or in challenging yourself to higher standards. You'll give up easily, not trying to stretch your capabilities in exams. In this case, you don't value your abilities highly enough to step out and achieve your academic goals.

You must also expand on your idea of where you think you belong. If you think of yourself as an average student who does just enough to pass, just passing is the outcome you'll achieve. However, if you can raise your standards and hold strong ideas about them in your mind, you'll activate your mind to behave in more resourceful ways of learning.

When your self-esteem around learning is high, you know what you're worth. You believe you can receive whatever grades you're aiming for, because you have the confidence to step out and learn new material, overcome setbacks, and persevere in the face of difficulties.

To enhance your self-esteem, you must find ways to raise your academic self-image. Like self-efficacy, you can enhance your self-esteem by setting goals that you can break into smaller tasks. When you witness yourself achieving each task, you start to feel worthy of going for greater goals. These tips can help:

- Acknowledge every little success. With every positive assignment and test result, deliberately dwell on the positive feelings of success.

- Use affirmative, encouraging, positive self-talk to take credit for your successes.

- Collect projects and papers that received good grades and positive comments from your teachers and e-mails from friends and bosses, and put them in a "feel good" folder. Then, if you have a setback, pull the folder out and remind yourself how good you are, how smart you are, and how capable you are.

Follow these guidelines and, in time, you'll enhance your self-image and your personal standards and expectations.

Modeling Yourself on High-Performance Students

In order to start believing you're capable in academic areas, you need to deliberately develop your academic self-image. A good way to achieve this goal is to gather information about the thinking strategies and behavior of students who are already performing at high academic levels. If you model, copy, or imitate their thinking and behavior, you can achieve similar results.

Try interviewing a high-performing student you know who's happy to talk about how she prepares for exams. In your interview, ask some of these questions:

- ✔ Do you see yourself as being a good student? Do you think it helps?

- ✔ Do you have high expectations for good results? How do these expectations influence your preparation?

- ✔ Are you aware of any positive self-talk you use when preparing for exams?

- ✔ What things do you think enabled you to get so good at [subject]?

- ✔ What specific practical strategies do you use to prepare for [subject] exams?

- ✔ What memory techniques do you use?

- ✔ How much time do you spend preparing for [subject] exams?

- ✔ How do you prepare mentally for [subject] exams?

- ✔ How long can you concentrate when preparing for [subject] exams?

- ✔ How do you eliminate distractions? Where do you study?

- ✔ Do you get exam anxiety? If so, how do you cope with it?

- ✔ What do you do to relax around exam time?

- ✔ What social support do you have to help you academically? Family? Friends?

- ✔ Do you think it helps to hang around with friends with similar academic aspirations?

  ✔ Do you implement any learning-style strengths?

  ✔ Do you play music when you study? Does it help?

You can add to this list by writing your own questions that you think may help you understand what high-performing students think and do. Then start copying their preparation strategies.

Developing Academic Goals

One way to turn positive thinking into action is to set goals. Do you know what you want in terms of academic goals? Can you see yourself preparing effectively and performing better at exams?

Set goals that are just ahead of your current ability, imprint these into your memory, and allow your conscious mind to lead the way. Many people aim for results based on their current appraisal of themselves, but the problem with this is that you're limited to your current motivation and creativity to achieve your goals. How much larger could your results be if you didn't have to know how you would achieve them? Let your creative mind do the work for you, and let it uncover how you can achieve the goals you set.

Deciding what you want is an essential thinking strategy for any life goal you set because

  ✔ Goals help you clarify and focus your thinking towards what you want. When you aim for a goal, you can tell when you're on or off track during the process of achieving it.

  ✔ Setting goals stimulates your awareness, telling your brain what's important out of the abundant information it receives every day.

  ✔ You become dissatisfied with your current reality, which engages your mind to make a change by causing cognitive dissonance (for a definition of cognitive dissonance, see "Conceptualizing Your Memory of You" earlier in this chapter).

  ✔ Repeating goals to make them the most dominant pictures in your mind imprints your memory to work towards them. I cover how to use repetition to your advantage in "Writing Affirmations: Declaring Your Intentions" and "Using Your Mind's Eye: Visualizing Success" later in this chapter.

Never make a goal without immediately doing something to kick-start it. Think of one thing that you can do right now that will move you towards your academic goal — right now, write it down and commit to it here. No matter how small, take action now!

Setting goals helps you stay on track

When you identify where you are now — perhaps your current academic standard in a particular subject, and where you want to be (your goal of a higher grade) — you can discover whether you're on track. This process is called your *teleological nature*.

Teleological means "purposeful design" and is a creative thinking process. Just like the autopilot on an airplane that gathers feedback from its environment to see whether it's on course or off course, you can figure out how to do the same process more consciously.

A good way to make use of your teleological nature is to keep a record of all your grades from assignments and tests for each subject throughout the year, and plot your results on a line graph. This process shows you whether you're improving. At the end of the developing line graph, place your ideal final result boldly marked at the date you want to reach it. As you move towards your goal and notice you're falling behind where you know you need to be, the dissatisfaction (dissonance) can cause your thinking to engage and self-correct to get you back on track. You may find yourself inventing better and faster ways to study for tests to get those grades up.

Setting goals stimulates your awareness

Having goals lets your brain know what's of value. Information that's perceived to be of value helps activate your brain's selection process that allows you to notice what matches it. (Chapter 2 covers your brain and how it learns.)

You experience your brain's attention system working when you decide you want something, say a new bike or car, and suddenly you start seeing what you want everywhere, whereas you didn't notice it in the past. The goal creates the value that causes the item to be of significance and noticed by your brain.

In the same way, deciding on a goal to raise your academic standards helps your brain search for clues in your environment. You'll hear people talking about how they're preparing for exams. You'll start to notice information on strategies that enhance exam performance — such as a flyer on a notice board inviting you to an exam review session or an ad for an online seminar — maybe even mine at www.passingexams.co.nz!

After you decide what you want, you start to see it all around you!

Setting goals motivates your mind

Setting a goal to be, do, or have something better tends to make people dissatisfied with their current situation. This dissatisfaction is actually an important process to help engage your mind to work for you. Because, in principle, human beings like order, and when you set a goal, you're throwing your system out of order. You're deliberately creating a dissonance between where you are now and where you want to be.

Your mind doesn't like dissonance. It wants to fix the problem and strives to restore order in the direction of the most dominant imprinted beliefs about yourself. If the most dominant self-images you hold are actually pictures of what you want — your goal — you'll find yourself becoming motivated and finding creative ways to reach it.

When I was halfway through my psychology degree, I won an award for excellence for doing well in sociology. My truth changed from being "maybe I can achieve this academic goal" to "I know I can achieve this academic goal." I found that I had a lot more motivation and drive. I turned off the television when I needed to study, whereas previously it was always a welcome distraction. I developed creative ways to study more effectively. I even designed a process to plan, write, and memorize essays for assignments and exams that I called essay route maps (covered in Chapter 10). This was my mind's creativity working for me towards achieving my goal.

Writing Affirmations: Declaring Your Intentions

Affirmations are positive statements of intent that steer you towards success by

- ✔ **Deliberately imprinting your memory:** When you repeat a phrase that defines what you want, it helps generate an internal mental movie of you being or having what you want. This movie imprints your memory.

- ✔ **Silencing any negative self-talk:** When your life is in a state of flux, or you're not yet familiar with the new behavior you're conditioning, writing down and saying affirmations replaces doubts with positive self-talk.

Prior to using affirmations, when I was preparing for exams, I would feel quite nervous. Before going into the exam, I would tell my friends how nervous I felt and that I hoped I could remember everything I had prepared because, right then, my mind was blank. Later, when I learned to use affirmations and sometimes started falling back into the old anxiety pattern, I would repeat: "I am clear, calm, and confident. Everything I need is coming to me now." This silenced the negative self-talk and helped me relax. As a result, I didn't have a problem with nervousness or memory blocks again.

When you're writing affirmations for conditioning your goals into your memory, you can consider using a number of guidelines. To write affirmations for a goal, follow these two steps:

1. **Identify and write down a problem or difficulty you're having that you believe is holding you back.**

   For example, exam anxiety is a common problem and you might write, "I get really nervous during the exam and find I can't remember what I studied."

2. **Write down the opposite of this difficulty — what you want.**

   Your response is the words you can use in an affirmation: "I am clear, calm, and confident during my exams."

Affirmation statements that you can use to help condition your mind to prepare and pass exams with ease include:

- ✔ I am good at studying!
- ✔ I love the way I am motivated to review before tests!
- ✔ I feel clear, calm, and confident leading up to these exams.
- ✔ I retain this information effortlessly.
- ✔ My recall is amazing!
- ✔ I am doing brilliantly!
- ✔ Yes, I got the grade I want!
- ✔ All the information is coming to me now.

Another way to write affirmations for your goals is to simply use your imagination to picture how you want your future to be and write it down. If you know that you're at a certain grade level and you want to raise your standards, write a statement that puts you at the higher standard now. If you've consistently been a B student and you want to raise the bar, begin affirming: "I am an A-grade student."

It's important that the words you use generate mental pictures and feelings. If you can't see and feel your goal as a real possibility, then bring your aspiration back a notch or two. Perhaps affirm: "I am a high B-grade student." When that becomes reality, begin affirming the next level you want to achieve.

These additional pointers can help you write effective affirmation statements:

- ✔ Because you're working to modify your self-image as if it describes who you are now, write your affirmations in the first person, present tense: "I am ...," "I have ...," and so on.

- ✔ Make your affirmation statements positive and action oriented. "I hate not feeling calm when I go into the exam" isn't a good affirmation. It creates a picture and feeling of nervousness, not calmness. "I feel clear, calm, and confident during exams" is a much better affirmation.

- ✔ Try not to compare yourself to others when you write affirmations. "I am smart like Jenny" isn't a good affirmation. "I love the way I absorb information easily" is better.

✔ Write your affirmations on small cards and carry them in your pocket. The more accessible they are, the better, because you want to use them every day.

✔ Use visual cues as reminders to do your affirmations: Fridge notes, your computer screen saver, your phone's profile screen, sticky notes posted around the house. You can also record your affirmations on a portable audio player and play them when you're exercising.

✔ Use affirmations when you're relaxed. Your body relaxes naturally when you're going to sleep or when you awake in the morning. You can also do a deliberate relaxation exercise to help make your mind more impressionable. This slows your brainwaves to the ideal learning state, called alpha state. (To find out more about accessing the alpha brainwave state, see Chapter 5.)

Using Your Mind's Eye: Visualizing Success

Writing affirmation statements and saying the words send powerful messages to your mind, but you also need to visualize the pictures and feelings you want the words to generate. Visualization with emotion is the real power behind imprinting your memory for success. Use your imagination to create vivid pictures and strong emotions when you think of your goals. Athletes often practice their sports mentally; visualization is equally helpful in improving your exam performance.

Research shows that visualization techniques are helpful because they create the neural patterns that help astrocytes track, map, and automate your thinking and behavior to help you achieve your best performance. Two-thirds of brain activity is the same whether your behavior is real or imagined. Because you don't take enough tests to wire in an ideal nonconscious response, visualization (mental rehearsal) is perfectly suited for this situation.

You use two types of visualization techniques to prepare for exams:

- ✔ **Process visualization:** With process visualization, you imagine yourself being and doing all the things that enable you to achieve your goal. For example, you imagine yourself sitting at your study desk and working through your notes, free from distractions and enjoying your ability to concentrate well.

- ✔ **Outcome visualization:** Outcome visualization is imagining yourself with the outcome you want on the day of your exam. You see yourself in the exam room, feeling calm and confident, writing furiously and smiling as you know everything you need to answer the questions. You may even want to see yourself receiving your ideal grade later on.

Spend 15 minutes a day in the weeks leading up to your exams using visualization to mentally rehearse how you want both the process and outcome of your exam preparation to unfold.

Sometimes people say: "I can't visualize. I don't see pictures in my head." Visualization doesn't have to be visual in the literal sense. If you don't see pictures clearly in your head, your brain may process information more easily through sound or feeling channels. Try verbalizing what you would see and feel. For example, for your outcome visualization, say,

> "I see myself in the exam room. My friends are sitting around me. I look really calm and confident as I begin writing quickly and easily."

As you recite what you want to see, also try to generate the feeling of being there and literally feeling calm and confident.

You need to relax before you begin visualizing. When your mind and body are relaxed, your brain is far more receptive to the conditioning you want to instill through visualization. The ideal times to visualize are just when you're about to go to sleep and again when you're waking in the morning. At these times, your brain has naturally accessed the ideal learning state known as alpha state (for more on alpha state, see Chapter 5).

Just do it!

Words don't teach — experience teaches, so just do it! Aiming to achieve your personal best is a mindset that takes effort and time to develop. Thinking strategies such as positive self-talk, writing down goals, and using visualization are learned habits. After you nail these techniques for learning, you can apply them to other areas of your life: Your relationships, your health, and your work.

Sometimes it can be difficult to take action — especially when the task is to study for exams, because you associate it with negative conditioning: "It's so boring," "I can't be bothered." or "I have to do it." Try these techniques to help you take action:

✔ **Clarify your purpose for studying.** What is your real goal? What's the big *why* behind this goal? When you get a strong sense of why you want to do it, staying focused becomes easier — especially when the going gets tough. Creating value in anything you want to achieve is a key component to making your brain receptive to learning.

✔ **Turn your *have to* into *want to*.** Say to yourself right now "I don't have to study for my exams." How does it feel when you say this? Say it a few times. Believe it; you have a choice. No one is making you do this — not your parents, employer, or teachers — only you can decide to do it or not. Now consider the flip side of this decision and the consequences. Think through what would happen if you don't study. Will you pass or fail, waste time or money? Now that you have a choice, will you decide you don't want these consequences? What are the positive benefits of making this choice?

The answers to these questions will help you turn your *have to* into a *want to*. Ask yourself, "Could I study effectively for this exam?" Then "Would I study effectively now that I have the option?" Finally, ask yourself, "When will I take action?" In other words — when is now a good time?

Part II
Relaxing Comes First

TIP

Five Reasons Why Relaxation is a Key Study Tool

- Adopting relaxation techniques will slow your brainwaves down to the alpha range, which is an ideal mental state to review and retain information.

- Allocating time for relaxation improves your overall life balance, health, and wellbeing during exam time.

- Relaxing between study sessions helps reduce neural system fatigue.

- Learning how to relax is an instantly effective exam-anxiety coping strategy.

- Allowing yourself to relax and have fun helps improve your morale during exam time.

Learning to relax is essential for effective exam preparation. Check out a free online article about how to relax at www.dummies.com/extras/passingexams.

In this part...

- ✔ Access your ideal learning state — alpha state — for improved learning.
- ✔ Develop a do-it-yourself alpha relaxation technique.
- ✔ Explore a variety of relaxation techniques and fun activities to help improve your life balance.
- ✔ Become familiar with mental rehearsal techniques to help cope with exam anxiety.
- ✔ Manage your study time and reduce your stress levels.

Chapter 5

Exploring the Power of Relaxation

*P*erhaps you're wondering what relaxation has to do with learning. Relaxation techniques are important to both learning and studying for two reasons: Firstly, they allow your brainwaves to slow down to access alpha state — the electrical frequency that allows your brain to be more receptive to what you notice — and secondly, they help reduce the mental, emotional, and physical stress that often occurs around exam time.

In this chapter, I explore the role relaxation plays in learning and reviewing, and show you how to get quickly into alpha state — your ideal learning state. When you understand the effect this brainwave frequency has on learning, you'll also see the value it has for all kinds of personal development.

Making Time for the Fun Stuff

Exams can be very stressful, and the pressure you put on yourself (or get from significant others) to do well can actually hinder your progress. Many students have told me they've given up all their fun activities to focus on exams. I did it myself! The problem with this is that without the fun stuff, you build stress because you're studying all the time, and stress limits learning!

You need fun stuff in your life to function properly so that you remain relaxed and receptive to learning.

Your brain releases *endorphins* (your body's natural feel-good chemical) when you're relaxed and having fun. It also releases the chemical *acetylcholine*, which has been linked to helping improve memory and learning. (For more information on how your brain works, refer to Chapter 2.)

Accelerated learning teacher and author Colin Rose (his books are online at www.acceleratedlearning.com) describes an experiment conducted in 50 different United States schools designed to test the fun theory. Taking into account brain research into neurochemical responses to fun, the schools introduced one hour of humor, music, and movement each day. By the end of the year, the results showed a 23 percent increase in academic performance!

Relaxation improves learning! Don't stop having fun, and find creative ways to relax as often as you can during the build-up to exams. (For a basic relaxation technique, see "Developing your own alpha relaxation technique" later in this chapter. I show you other ways to relax in Chapter 6.)

Accessing Alpha State (Your Ideal Learning Zone)

Ideally, all learning takes place when you're in a relaxed state and primarily accessing alpha brainwaves. In *alpha state* — the brainwave frequency that produces a feeling of relaxed alertness — your brainwaves slow to around 8 to 12 hertz (Hz), and you become primed to receive information. This is because relaxation helps your brain's information selection process to stimulate your attention more freely. (I discuss brainwaves and other brain functions in Chapter 2.)

If you continue to relax deeply, you can access theta state, (4 to 7 Hz). Scientists believe that this slower brainwave activity can help you draw on greater inspiration and creativity.

Interestingly, whenever you're feeling anxious or stressed, such as during an exam, your brain releases chemicals that interfere with memory and prevent information from being recalled — producing that tip-of-the-tongue feeling people describe as a *memory block, brain cramp*, and other colorful conditions.

However, if at this point you implement a relaxation exercise that generates alpha brainwaves, your memory improves.

Developing your own alpha relaxation technique

You can deliberately access alpha state by using relaxation techniques. For example, before you start a review or study session, close your eyes, take a few deep breaths and, as you breathe out, tell yourself to, "Relax ... relax ... relax." Your thinking directly influences your nervous system so that as you affirm these words, your body relaxes as well. You can use this simple technique in an exam if you do get a memory block.

For a full script on how to access alpha state before a study session, turn to Appendix B at the end of this book. The best way to use the script in Appendix B is to record it on an audio device and listen to it frequently. Take note that in this script you create a trigger movement to help you access alpha state every time you activate the movement. This is called an *anchor* and is used in *neuro-linguistic programming* (NLP), a brain and behavior modification science originally developed by personal and professional development experts Richard Bandler and John Grinder. After you get the hang of anchoring your trigger (through practice or repetition), you'll be able to get to a relaxed state within seconds. Use this script before any exam review session.

Exploring self-hypnosis and mental rehearsal

Self-hypnosis (also called autosuggestion) and *mental rehearsal* (repeatedly imagining a new behavior) are two ways you can independently recondition your thoughts to be more empowering. Use the following mental rehearsal technique (which combines self-hypnosis) to think and imagine your ideal exam performance:

1. **Start with a real desire to change a limiting belief you hold about yourself, and a desire to use this mental rehearsal approach to improve your exam performance.**

   For example, you may have a chronic fear of exam situations that you know limits your performance. Your exam results may not reflect your true academic potential.

2. **Think about your perceived problem and needs, and then work out a script that replaces negative thoughts with positive suggestions to install in your mind.**

   For example, when you think about being in an exam, see and feel yourself being clear, calm, and confident. You can say the words, "I feel clear, calm, and confident" and "I recall everything I reviewed with ease."

3. **Implement the relaxation technique that helps you access alpha state.**

   Refer to "Developing your own alpha relaxation technique" earlier in this chapter. Verbally recite the whole process of relaxation.

4. **Finish with positive suggestions.**

   To help you do this, you can use the mental rehearsal script I provide in Appendix B.

Tricking your brain into learning

Did you know that your brain doesn't know the difference between what's real and what's imagined? For example, if I asked you to imagine holding a rosy red apple in your hand right now, could you do it? Could you see the shape, texture and color of the apple — even get a sense of its weight in your hand? Now imagine taking a bite from the apple. What's your response? Did you get an increase of saliva in your mouth?

This little exercise shows how well your mind and body are integrated. When you think about something, even if it's not real, you get a physiological response in your body.

So how can you use this idea to help improve your learning? You can use your imagination to trick your brain into being more receptive to learning.

Remember, value and relaxation help your brain's information selection process to be more receptive. To create value, imagine that you've just finished a review session. Ask yourself what benefits you get from learning and studying? The more you can imagine the positive benefits you'll receive (as if you have them now), the more your brain will be receptive to learning.

To improve relaxation, simply imagine yourself in the most relaxing place you could ever find — a beach scene, mountain scene, or someplace close to your heart. As you see yourself in this relaxing place, try to feel yourself actually there, actually relaxing. Breathe into that scene. Your brain, not knowing the difference between what's real and imagined, will signal your body to relax.

Record the process and listen to it repeatedly. As you listen to the recording, the new suggestions are imprinted into your memory. Writing affirmations and visualizing success are other ways you can condition your memory. (For some pointers on these, refer to Chapter 4.)

Researchers have discovered that students who use mental rehearsal as an exam preparation technique perform better on exams than those who don't. Mental rehearsal is also a common preparation approach used in professional motivation programs, which I talk more about in the next section.

Using Personal Development Programs

Professional services and programs that focus on positive behavior modifications offer huge benefits for students. Some specialize in improving your learning abilities and study techniques.

Some resources you may be interested in include:

- **Neuro-associative conditioning:** Anthony Robbins, a well-respected international writer, teacher, and personal development coach, uses neuro-associative conditioning in his self-development programs, Personal Power and Get the Edge. *Neuro-associative conditioning* involves reconditioning the patterns of thoughts you've wired into your brain so that your thinking, and consequently your behavior, can improve. The technique involves going into alpha state and identifying limiting beliefs, then interrupting old thought patterns and repeatedly conditioning them to be more positive. You can find more about Robbins's techniques on his website, www.anthonyrobbins.com.

- **Paraliminal audio CDs:** These special technology-based recordings bypass your conscious, thinking mind to imprint a positive message into your memory. In the United States, the Learning Strategies Corporation (www.learningstrategies.com) produces a whole range of resources that can help you to condition your mind and body into more resourceful states. From stopping smoking to rapid reading, these resources aim to develop your personal and professional effectiveness.

✔ **Hypnosis:** A therapist trained in hypnosis can condition you by implanting positive ideas into your memory while you're in a relaxed state. This can help you literally deactivate any limiting beliefs affecting your learning or exam preparation so that you can react and respond in more resourceful ways.

To find a trained hypnotherapist in your area, search the Internet for your national hypnotherapist association, and check its national register.

I believe students underuse professional services and programs. If you're experiencing difficulties in learning or preparing for exams or want to build on the methods I offer in this book, seek outside help from a trained hypnotherapist or an educational psychologist. You can also contact me through my website at www.passingexams.co.nz where I offer coaching using Skype.

Chapter 6

Finding Ways to Relax

· ·

In This Chapter

▶ Understanding what exercise can do for you

▶ Relaxing through music

▶ Stretching and breathing techniques

▶ Dealing with your emotions

▶ Making time for study and play

▶ Keeping your life in balance

· ·

C lose your eyes, take a deep breath and relax. Sound good to you? How often do you deliberately allow yourself to relax — to intentionally rest? Probably not often enough.

Keeping the balance between doing and being, or activity and rest, is the key to a happy and successful life, yet so many people, myself included at times, spend most of their time doing and very little time just being.

Relaxation plays a key role in learning because it helps your brain pay attention to the information you gather through your senses. Relaxation is also believed to improve neural and astrocyte communication in response to the type of neurotransmitters being produced. (Chapter 5 explains the importance of relaxation.)

In this chapter, I suggest a range of relaxation exercises that you can incorporate — not only during study times, but any time — to help keep your life in balance. These exercises allow you to relax through stretching and breathing, meditation, trips to nature, and professional bodywork sessions, through better time management, and by keeping your life enriched.

Exercising for Relaxation

Have you ever wondered why you find yourself automatically relaxing when you go for a walk in nature? Scientifically speaking, the Earth has an electromagnetic frequency of around 7.8 hertz, which is also the low end of human alpha state frequency, the ideal state for studying. So, like a tuning fork that matches the vibration of another tuning fork, your brain, when taken for a walk in nature, slows its rate from the beta range (which can hold tension in the body) to the alpha state, and harmonizes with the natural setting you're in. (I talk about alpha and beta states in Chapter 5.)

For example, if you spend hours in front of a computer screen without a break, you're likely to feel agitated. Your computer emits a frequency in the high beta range. Your brain harmonizes with this frequency, and the high level of prolonged mental vibration causes tension in your body and mind.

Considering this, when you're required to spend long hours in front of a computer screen or in a high-tech environment, make sure you take lots of breaks and walks in the park.

Similarly, exercising more frequently around exam time is a great way to burn off unwanted stress. Running, walking, cycling, swimming, and many other sports are great ways to keep your body and mind in balance.

Balancing study time with relaxation time is very important around exam time. Without relaxation, your body and mind become tense, and tension is not conducive to good learning or review. When exams are looming, frequent relaxation time keeps your body and mind in balance, and your motivation, concentration, and interest intact.

Exploring Sound and Music

Music can be a powerful aid in the relaxation process. If done correctly, you can use music to help you access your alpha state effortlessly.

Many accelerated learning techniques offer classical music (usually baroque by Bach, Handel, or Vivaldi) as background music when reviewing for exams. They suggest that your brain will match the rhythm of this music, slow your brainwaves, release *endorphins* (pleasure chemicals), and relax your body for receptive learning.

Try music as a relaxation tool next time you sit down to study:

- ✔ **Soft, classical baroque music:** Keep in mind that it's not important to like this type of music (although don't listen if you discover that the music annoys you). Simply think of the music as a tool to help you improve your ability to receive information while you're reviewing test materials.

- ✔ **Meditation music:** Classical harp, the sounds of nature, or voices chanting are all available to help increase relaxation.

- ✔ **High-tech, alpha-inducing music:** The holosynch soundtrack produced by the Centerpointe Research Institute in the United States (www.centerpointe.com) is one example. It sounds like a repetitive drone, but actually enables positive brain entrainment, a concept I explore in Chapter 2.

You can download some free relaxation music from my website at www.passingexams.co.nz.

Two ways you can use relaxing music to help you study are

- ✔ **Active concerts:** Someone verbally recites review notes in time to music (this can be recorded). You listen to the words while the music enhances your receptivity.

- ✔ **Passive concerts:** You record your review notes with music playing softly in the background. You listen to the music while you absorb the spoken study notes subconsciously.

Alternatively, you can play any relaxing music in the background while you study. However, your favorite contemporary music is not ideal, because it may draw your attention to the rhythm, beat, and lyrics, and away from your reviewing. However, if your favorite music is so familiar that you don't really pay it any attention — and it doesn't incite you to sing along — then listening to it should be fine.

Your brain can't consciously turn its attention to two things simultaneously. If you're listening to your music and singing along or paying attention to the lyrics, any study efforts are a waste of time. Any music you play must not be the type that draws your attention to it.

Free creative movement to music is another wonderful relaxation exercise. Put on some music that feels appropriate for the mood you're in. Close your eyes and let your body move with the music — but not to it. In other words, your body knows how it wants to move and that may not be to the beat or rhythm of the music. Let your soul express itself. You can be lying on your back, simply moving a hand, or performing any other movement that feels right in that moment.

Stretching Out, Breathing Out

The human nervous system contains two parts that perform distinct roles:

- ✔ **Sympathetic nervous system:** Responsible for engaging your mind and body to respond to the demands of the environment you're in. If that environment is physically and mentally demanding for a prolonged period of time, you begin to hold tension.

- ✔ **Parasympathetic nervous system:** Designed to bring you back to homeostasis — a state of stability or balance.

The problem is, if you hold tension in your body for a long time, it becomes embedded in your muscles and tendons. You may think you feel relaxed, but in fact you're still holding tension you're unaware of. By deliberately performing stretching and breathing exercises you can release that built-up tension in your body.

You can employ a number of great general relaxation exercises immediately to help you relax during your day.

I love exercises that help invoke a relaxed state or extend my capabilities, and you can use a variety of techniques to experience a shortcut to relaxation and concentration:

- ✔ **Relaxation:** One simple exercise is to place the palms of your hands over your eyes to create darkness. This tricks the brain into thinking it's nighttime and signals that it's time to sleep. Now repeat to yourself a relaxing affirmation — for example, "Peace ... peace ... peace ..." Remember to breathe deeply and feel your body relax.

- ✔ **Concentration:** This exercise helps you realize just how much time you spend thinking thoughts you may not even be aware of. Look at the secondhand turning on your watch or other clock. Concentrate only on the seconds, and see how long you can go before your mind thinks about something else. Using this exercise to improve your attention span is helpful because researchers believe good attention, like relaxation, is important for learning and preparation for tests.

The following sections offer some easily learned practical examples. You can also consider more structured alternatives, such as yoga or tai chi classes.

The quick-relax technique

Sit in a comfortable position with your hands on your lap, one cupping the other and facing upwards. Close your eyes, and roll your eyeballs up — imagine you're looking at the center of your forehead (this is the position your eyes move to when you're sleeping and doing so tricks your brain into thinking it's time to relax for sleep). Hold this position for the duration of the exercise.

Breathe deeply into your stomach without expanding your chest. Inhale through your nose, and gently out through your mouth. Feel your weight in the chair; pay attention for a moment to any tension, aches, or pains in your body. Let them go as you breathe out.

Now visualize a memory of a time in your life when you felt incredibly relaxed. Perhaps invoke a holiday scene. If you can't recall a relaxed memory, picture the most relaxing time you can imagine. Perhaps you're sitting in a natural hot pool? Bring in as much detail as possible. As you visualize this scene, start affirming to yourself: "Relax ... relax ... relax" over and over, slowly and deeply. Feel your body becoming more and more relaxed as you go through this process.

Because of the body–mind link, as you relax your body, your brainwaves begin to slow down too. This is what you want in order to enter your subconscious mind. After a few minutes you should reach a reasonable level of relaxation. Now return to the room by counting from one to five and slowly opening your eyes.

You can reach this state of relaxation again, simply by sitting in a comfortable position, cupping your hands, breathing deeply, imagining your relaxing situation, and affirming to yourself the words, "Relax ... relax ... relax." The more often you do this, the more easily and quickly you'll find that space in the future.

Practice this relaxation technique for five to ten minutes a day for at least 30 days. This helps to make the technique habitual and become a part of your life.

Mindful breathing

Have you noticed that when you're concentrating, feeling nervous, or afraid, you take shorter breaths? Mindful breathing is a vital tool to help reduce these stressful situations.

A good breathing exercise is to register as you inhale and exhale. Pay attention to the rhythm and flow of your breathing. Where does the air fill first — your chest or stomach region? How long is the gap between breaths? Is it longer on the inhale or exhale?

When you're in a stressful situation, take a number of deep breaths. Try to breathe longer on the exhale than you did when you breathed in. Count to yourself — up to four seconds on the inhale and up to eight seconds on the exhale (or any count using a one-to-two ratio). Release the tension and emotions you're feeling with your exhale. Make some movement and noise too, if it feels appropriate.

Body balance

Sometimes, practicing some body-awareness exercises helps you to relax.

How long can you keep your body still? Lie on your back with your arms and legs slightly apart. Close your eyes, breathe deeply, and imagine your whole body relaxing. Move in your mind's eye through your body from your feet to your head, relaxing each part as you go.

When you feel as relaxed as you can get, stay lying there as still as you can, for at least three minutes. If your body becomes tense or fidgety, stop the exercise and try again later.

The five-minute morning stretch

How often do you consciously stretch and breathe when you get up in the morning? By gearing up your body in this way, you feel brighter and more alert, ready to face the day.

Try the following exercise:

1. **Sit on the floor with your legs stretched out in front of you. Take some deep breaths, right down into the pit of your stomach.**

   Put your awareness into your breathing throughout the exercise, to help you stay focused in the present moment.

2. **Move your ankles, stretching them forwards and backwards. Wriggle your knees up and down.**

3. **Move your shoulders up and down, then loosely move your arms around.**

4. **Rotate your wrist joints. Raise your arms above your head and clasp your hands.**

   Feel the stretch in your shoulders.

5. **Move your head from side to side, then up and down, stretching your neck.**

6. **Rub your face and scalp with your hands.**

7. **Open your eyes wide and move them from side to side, then up and down.**

8. **Move your jaw muscles.**

   Try making some noise while you do this.

9. **Bring your left foot up to your pelvis and lean forward over your right leg.**

   Hold the stretch for 15 seconds. Then do the same on the other side.

10. **Spread your legs wide out in front of you and lean slightly forward, stretching the inner thighs.**

11. **Return your legs out in front and lean forward over them, gently stretching your lower back.**

12. **Bring your right leg up by bending your knee and place your right foot over your left leg at the knee. Turn your upper body around to the right, stretching by placing your left arm against the outside of your right knee.**

    Do the same with your other leg, twisting to the left.

13. **Now release, relax, and turn over, and lie on your stomach.**

14. **Arch your back by raising your upper body with your arms.**

15. **Now stretch your back the other way by raising your buttocks up to now stand in an inverted V on your hands and feet.**

    This pose is known as downward-facing dog in yoga. Feel the stretch in your calves.

    Let your head hang loosely between your shoulders. Breathe deeply, lower, relax, and then repeat three times.

16. **You're finished stretching. Sit quietly on your knees for a few moments, breathing deeply again and being aware of your body.**

You can also perform stretching and breathing exercises when you're not at home. Find a moment at work or at school to shake out your arms and legs, or stretch your neck and back. You can do these simple exercises even while you're sitting down, at a desk, or in the car (provided the vehicle's stationary if you're the driver). Try to become more in tune with your body and what it needs. Your body can tell you what it needs — if you find time and are still enough to listen.

Meditation

Some people believe that meditation involves spending hours sitting in serious contemplation or humming "om" like some guru on a mountain in India. But people practice meditation by simply walking in the countryside. Any quiet time that frees your mind from thoughts and worries can be classed as meditation.

If even only for a few minutes, try to clear your thoughts and bring your mind to a resting state. Being totally focused in the present moment calms your mind and brings in a stillness that can also help alleviate stress.

Meditation classes that can help you relax are held in most communities. To find out about meditation classes in your region, visit your local library, natural healing center, whole foods store, citizens advice bureau, or gym.

Releasing Unwanted Emotions

Unwanted, pent-up emotions can stifle your ability to relax. The Sedona Method (www.sedona.com) is one personal development system that helps you work through emotions. It involves asking yourself key questions to help you release them.

One way to apply the method is to imagine that someone really made you angry. Although you hated feeling this way, you just couldn't help yourself. You can release your anger by following these steps:

1. **Ask yourself: Could I let this anger go? Notice how you feel.**

   Your mind does a quick cost–benefit analysis and, at some point, you're able to make a decision that you could let the feeling go.

2. **Ask yourself: Would I let this anger go? Notice how you feel.**

   The question takes your thinking to a new level. Your brain scans your values, beliefs, and attitudes, does another cost–benefit analysis, and decides what to do. At this point you're likely to think that you're willing to let the feeling go.

3. **Now ask yourself: When?**

   You'll most likely discover that "now" is the answer.

4. **Close your eyes, take a deep breath, and decide, stating to yourself, "I let this anger go now."**

   That's all there is to it!

Another approach you can try to release unwanted emotions is to simply take the attitude that you don't have good or bad feelings — just feelings.

Give yourself permission. Allow yourself to feel those "bad" feelings. Your body and mind are good at holding on to negative emotions, especially if you don't allow them to surface. The best way to deal with them is to accept them and tell yourself that it's really okay to feel this way. Repeat this statement a number of times, "It's really okay to feel this way; it's really, really okay to feel this way; it's really, really, really okay to feel this way."

What happens next is that by allowing the feelings to pass through your mind and body, and by not blocking them, the opposite feelings begin to emerge. Feelings work through a unique paradox. What you resist, persists!

Blissing out with professional relaxation sessions

Treat yourself to regular relaxation sessions. For example, therapeutic massage or aromatherapy can do wonders to boost your self-esteem, self-confidence, and general outlook on life. Because your body and mind are so integrated, ensuring your body is relaxed has a positive effect on your thinking as well.

Juggling

Buy some juggling balls from the local toyshop and teach yourself this enjoyable hobby (I tell you how in Chapter 2). The process of juggling develops hand–eye coordination as well as body–mind coordination. By being totally focused in this enjoyable way, you free your mind from thinking stressful thoughts or worrying.

Managing Time

Time can be a big issue when it comes to keeping your life in balance. A lot of stress comes from feelings of not having enough time. Although relaxation is important to revising for exams, I suspect it's not high on your priorities list unless the other things you're required to do are sorted first.

Managing your time is more about managing your life. If you don't have your time organized, your life will be full of pressures.

Make a list of all the things that you have to do on a daily or weekly basis, then draw up a schedule similar to the one shown in Figure 6-1. Place each task in one of the four categories: Urgent, Not Urgent, Important, Not Important.

Ensure that you schedule studying for exams and taking a break from studying in the Important and Urgent quadrants. Choose an activity from the relaxation options I offer earlier in this chapter and add it to the schedule.

This method of prioritizing your tasks is very helpful in managing your time and your life. It can help you break the habit of spending time on activities that fall in the Not Urgent and Not Important quadrants.

	Urgent	**Not Urgent**
Important	History revision	Walk dog in park
Not Important		

Figure 6-1: Setting up your task list to prioritize what's important and what's urgent.

After you establish what's important to you and prioritize your tasks, don't forget to eliminate all unnecessary activities that you're doing during the build-up to exams.

Another time-management strategy is to spend a day or two keeping a log to determine how you spend your time. You may be surprised at how much time you're wasting on unnecessary activities. Next, create a chart similar to Figure 6-2, and list the time-wasting activities in the left-hand column, then jot down ways to eliminate them in the right-hand column.

Time wasters	*Strategy to fix*

Figure 6-2: Determining how you spend your time.

The key point is to take actions to reduce or eliminate interruptions that distract you from keeping your study time productive. For more information on eliminating distractions, turn to Chapter 3.

Planning how you're going to spend your review time is also useful. Research shows that more time spent on planning actually saves time when doing the activity.

In Appendix A, I provide daily and weekly planners you can copy. Use these to plan what you will do and when — but only after you've prioritized your tasks first, using the chart shown in Figure 6-1.

Scheduling relaxation time before exam time is very important. Relaxation keeps your body and mind in balance, and balance ensures productive reviewing and a productive life.

Enriching Your Life

Giving yourself plenty of time for fun and pleasure is the key to relaxation. Ask yourself these questions:

- ✔ How much joy do I have in my life?
- ✔ Do I have balance in my life, or am I spending all my time studying?
- ✔ Do I need to find new ways to enliven and entertain myself?
- ✔ What did I do for fun as a child? Fly kites or go to a ball game? Would I like to do these things again — to let my inner child free?

You could start a night class or take up a new hobby, just for fun — a good way to meet new and interesting people. Treat yourself to regular relaxation sessions. Get out and visit parks and the countryside more often and find more ways to appreciate your surroundings. Acquire a pet — a pet dog or cat can bring out the playful side in you. Invite friends over more often; or go out dancing. If you take time to think about it, you'll find plenty of ways to enrich your life.

Part III
Reviewing and Rewriting Your Notes

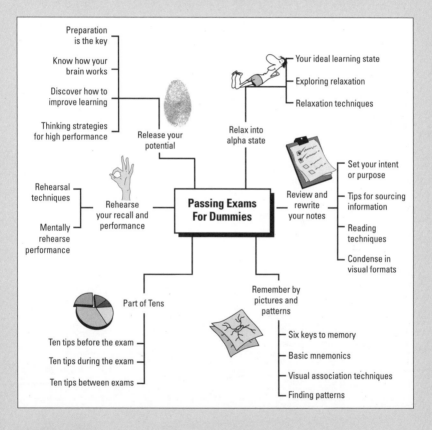

Preparation is the key

Know how your brain works

Discover how to improve learning

Thinking strategies for high performance

Release your potential

Your ideal learning state

Exploring relaxation

Relaxation techniques

Relax into alpha state

Rehearsal techniques

Rehearse your recall and performance

Mentally rehearse performance

Passing Exams For Dummies

Review and rewrite your notes

Set your intent or purpose

Tips for sourcing information

Reading techniques

Condense in visual formats

Part of Tens

Ten tips before the exam

Ten tips during the exam

Ten tips between exams

Remember by pictures and patterns

Six keys to memory

Basic mnemonics

Visual association techniques

Finding patterns

web extras

Condense your class notes into study notes catered to help memory retention. Check out a free essay route map technique at www.dummies.com/extras/passingexams.

In this part ...

✔ Practice setting academic intentions to direct and develop your study skills.

✔ Learn how to search and select the most important information you need to prepare for your exam.

✔ Understand the different review and reading techniques and how best to use them.

✔ Discover how to prepare effective study notes suitable for practicing your memory retention and recall.

✔ Use essay route maps to prepare content for assignment and exam essays.

Chapter 7

Knowing Your Academic Purpose

Do you know what your life purpose is at the moment? This is one of the most profound questions you can ask yourself. If you know what switches you on, gets you fired up and passionate, and drives you forward against adversity, you have clues to discovering your purpose.

Knowing your purpose can be a carefully worked-out personal statement, a vision of your ideal life, or a strong inner sense of why you're here. Whatever forms your purpose becomes a part of you; it's the core *why* factor in your life and can help you make day-to-day decisions, gently guiding you towards achieving your goals.

Just as your life purpose can guide you, an academic purpose can help you pass exams. In this chapter, I outline the importance of being clear about your academic purpose, and I show you how you can set intentions to direct and develop every aspect of your studies.

The emphasis in this chapter is to show you how to focus your intention on what you want to achieve within both short-term and long-term timeframes. When you understand exactly how intention works, you can start to use it deliberately.

Developing the Power of Intention

If you've ever explored the field of quantum physics, you know that everything is energy. Take a look around you right now. What do you see? A floor, walls, ceiling, tables, chairs, people, plants, animals, glass ... all seemingly solid, but made up of atoms and molecules (electrons, subatomic particles, subsubatomic particles, empty space) vibrating at different speeds, or frequencies, of energy.

As scientists explore reality at a quantum level, more and more evidence is surfacing that *all life* is connected by an invisible energy field, and this field is influenced by your clear and directed thoughts — your *intentions*.

Human beings can tune into and turn on this universal energy through the power of their deliberate intention. Your thoughts literally create your reality, and if you accept this, then your potential for bigger, better, and greater things in life can be governed by your deliberate intentions.

To begin exploring your intentions, consider these points to help you get to your intentions for

- ✔ **What you want to learn:** Can you spell out on paper the short-term and long-term goals you want to achieve?

- ✔ **Each exam you'll be undertaking:** What outcome do you want for each? Are you clear on your goals here?

- ✔ **Your exam preparation this week:** Have you set up a study schedule?

- ✔ **Your next review session:** Do you know exactly what material you want to cover in your next study hour?

This list offers ways of using deliberate intent to help you plan your future experience. Throughout the rest of this chapter, I look at ways you can apply your intent and influence your study sessions.

Whether for the long term or the very short term (say, within the next hour), by using your imagination to activate the power of deliberate intent, you can set in motion the unified field of energy that influences your reality and accomplish what you want.

Setting Your Intention for Each Study Session

Picture this: You're sitting at your desk, ready to review a load of information. Your books and folders are stacked around you and you look on them with a heavy feeling, thinking, "where do I begin?"

In many ways, this is a good question to ask yourself because by asking it, you set your mind to seeking the answer.

Here's what to do: State firmly to yourself the purpose your review session. For example, "In the next 50 minutes, I want to read through my English notes about that novel I studied last month, and retrieve all the key information I'll need to write an exam essay on characterization."

You need to be specific in your intention to get the desired outcome. In the following sections, I show you how.

Focusing on what you want

Try setting your intention by clearly defining the purpose of your next review session. When you state your intention firmly, focusing specifically on what you want to achieve, two things happen psychologically:

- ✔ **You pay attention:** You open your awareness to the task at hand. You're telling your brain to pay attention to information that's aligned with your intention, and discard information that isn't important (to discover how this happens, see "Telling your brain what should get through" in the following section). If you take a moment to set your intention before a study session, you can save hours of wasted study time spent aimlessly sifting through your notes in a muddle.

- ✔ **You avoid tension:** You place the idea — what you want to achieve — strongly in your mind. This helps stimulate energy and motivation to get the task done, and it reduces stress.

Relaxed and ready for learning

You can deliberately invoke a no-tension state by relaxing with a breathing technique (refer to Chapters 5 and 6). Coupled with a set intention, this allows you to place yourself in a ready state to review material.

Use an affirmation while you're breathing. For example, say, "I set my intention, focus my attention, and relax. I am ready to study!" This can help you get into the habit of using your intent before any review session.

When your intention is strong, you feel more enthusiastic, confident, and able to complete the task with ease. Your concentration and focus become tuned in and, with very little tension, you realize an hour has passed in what felt like a matter of minutes. You're in the flow.

Telling your brain what should get through

In Chapter 5, I discuss the use of relaxation techniques before beginning a study session. The reason for this is twofold:

- ✔ To help your brain become more receptive to the information you're about to study (for more information on how your brain's information selection process works, see Chapters 2 and 5)

- ✔ To help settle your nervous system during the pressure of exam time

So, you need to ensure that you're relaxed first (see my tip in the sidebar "Relaxed and ready for learning") before you apply your intent.

Setting your intention for a review session tells your brain what information to focus on and engages your attention to allow through only information that has significance right now. If information has no value (it's not aligned with your intention), it won't get through to your thinking brain to be processed.

Some short-term intentions you could apply to a 50-minute study session include

✔ I want to review Chapters 14–17 in my psychology text book and retrieve all key information I need for the short-answer questions for my next exam.

✔ I want to practice the science review questions three times, so that I know I understand them properly.

✔ I want to skim-read key points in my accounting notes so that I'm more familiar with the content before I do more in-depth studying tomorrow.

✔ I want to create mind maps highlighting all the key points that make up the likely World War II questions in my history exam.

Staying on target

If you have trouble maintaining concentration when preparing for exams, know that your intention can help you focus. Any intention set, no matter what the size or timeframe, can improve your effectiveness in that moment.

Authors Esther and Jerry Hicks (online at Abraham-Hicks Publications, www.abraham-hicks.com) use the term *segmented intent* in their book, *The Amazing Power of Deliberate Intent*, to describe using the power of intention to set up your day exactly how you want it to be — minute-by-minute, if need be. Here's a good example:

> You unexpectedly receive an important phone call. Ask the caller to hold for a moment while you quickly and deliberately set your intention, deciding how you want the call to go. You then resume the call with your intention set.

By using segmented intent when you study, you can plan your experiences so that your day-to-day life unfolds from the intentions you've outlined. Instead of taking life as it comes, you become the architect of your daily experience — designing, building, and shaping your life into a fuller expression of your greater purpose.

Sometimes, a visual cue helps you stay on purpose. For a little motivational cartoon that you can copy and place in your study space, go to Appendix C.

Setting Your Intention for Long-Term Goals

You may like to set long-term intentions. Although goals allow you to focus on the results you want, intentions focus you on the way you achieve those results.

Setting weekly intentions

Weekly intentions are a useful way of planning not only what you want to achieve, but also how you want your week to flow. For example, try setting an intention for the week ahead. On Sunday night, decide what you want to achieve during the week and how you want to go about it.

Sit in a chair and use your imagination to see yourself in the week ahead. What do you want to get done? How do you want to go about it? For example, you may want to prepare new condensed review notes for three subjects. Perhaps you're planning to keep Wednesday night free to go to the movies with a friend. You may also need to work on the weekend. After you have a clear vision of what you want to do and get accomplished, and when, bring in your feelings or emotions. See and feel yourself moving through your days with ease. As you study, see and feel yourself studying effortlessly and efficiently so that you have more time than you expected. Feel pleased with yourself. See and feel yourself having a good time with your friend on Wednesday evening, and then enjoying the way you interact with people at work on the weekend.

Finish your mental movie with a sense of expectation that your week will flow just as you intend. You can finish with the affirmation: If it's to be, it's up to me!

Setting monthly or yearly intentions

You can apply the process you use to set weekly intentions (covered in the preceding section) to set monthly or yearly intentions.

Take a few moments to set out how you see your month or year going. What do you want to achieve within this timeframe? Write down some goals for the month and year. For example, in the month leading up to exams, you may write, "I want to prepare for all my exams with ease. I have the energy and motivation to study and have confidence that my efforts will be rewarded with great results."

You can use these words to see yourself as the lead character in your own mental movie. When you say the words, see and feel yourself actually achieving your goals as your ideal month or year unfolds.

Another important thing to do is to run through your monthly intentions at least once a week. This allows you to keep yourself on track. As you get closer to the end of the month and realize you're not achieving what you intended, the time constraint builds a sense of tension in your system. Your mind doesn't like the tension and will look for ways to fix the problem. (I provide more information on how this works in the next section.)

Setting a time limit

Time plays a key role when you're studying for exams because in your mind you have so much to do in what feels like so little time. In Chapters 3 and 6, I provide some useful tips on exploring how you manage your time. Take a look at these chapters if you're feeling pressured by a lack of time.

Another aspect to working with time constraints is to first understand what happens psychologically when you set a time limit. Including a time limit with the intention you set prompts your energy and motivation, creativity, and problem-solving skills to increase as you draw closer to your deadline. Setting a time limit intensifies your motivation to get the task finished. Your mind says, "I've got 50 minutes to get this done. I better get to it!"

On the flip side, don't let a time limit cause excessive stress. Remember, focusing on what you want is more difficult if you're tense. A part of you needs to always be concerned with keeping your life in balance — a part of you needs to say, "If I don't get it done, it's not the end of the world!" In principle, however, setting a time limit is helpful because it can increase your motivation and creativity as your deadline approaches.

Preparing a time planner

To help you organize your time for reviewing and rewriting material, prepare a timetable so that you can see what needs to be done by when. In Chapter 14, I include a filled-out timetable that provides useful guidelines, whether you're in high school, university, or studying for a professional or certification exam.

Chapter 8

Reviewing Your Notes

. . . .

. . . .

*A*fter you switch on your brain with a relaxation exercise and set your deliberate intent for a study session (refer to Chapters 6 and 7), you can start reviewing your notes. This involves focusing on the information that's most likely to be on the text.

In this chapter, I outline a number of review strategies to help sort your notes and learning materials, and make the most of other resources that can help you pass exams. I also show you how to find material in addition to your course content. With an effective strategy to find extra information, you can save yourself hours of preparation time.

Sourcing Information

You're likely to gather a huge amount of information on each subject you study that may include class notes, photocopied material, computer printouts, course books, audio recordings, and more. Now it's time to search through them and determine what's important to review and what's not.

Deciding what you need to review

A great way to find out what questions you're likely to be asked in an exam is to obtain copies of the past year's exams. Look for patterns that can give you clues to the type of questions you may be asked for this year's exam.

If you can't get access to a previous year's exam questions, consider asking someone who might know — an older student, a teacher, a work colleague, or employer. Interrogate these people until you have a good idea of what's likely to be asked in the exam.

After speaking to others and discerning information from those in the know for ideas on the likely exam questions, a useful question to ask yourself while going over your course notes is, "If I could take my notes into the exam, which ones would I take?" You may find that as you browse through your notes, some of the information looks, sounds, or feels more important. At a nonconscious level, your memory is recalling these points in relation to the question you're probing it with. (Refer to Chapter 7 for tips on setting your intention.)

Paying attention at a review class

Often, a teacher or lecturer will set aside a special class to review likely exam content. Make sure you don't miss this class!

During pre-exam review sessions it's extremely helpful to be aware of your teacher's body language. Your teacher knows the content of the exam you're preparing for, but, for obvious reasons, isn't allowed to give away too much. However, because most communication received is non-verbal, the teacher may unwittingly give away clues without actually saying so in words. To increase your non-verbal awareness in a situation like this, consider these aspects:

- ✔ **Paralanguage:** This covers the sound of words as they're being spoken. Look for emphasis in volume, tone, pitch, and speech rate. If a certain point is important, paralanguage helps get the message across to you, without saying, "There will be specific questions on ...." Important points are usually communicated in a slow, firm, low voice.

- ✔ **Eye contact:** Notice where teachers place their eyes when speaking to the class. Intense, directed eye contact indicates an important point. Less important points elicit more relaxed, less focused eye contact.

- ✔ **Facial expressions and gestures:** A lot of emphasis on important points is often relayed through expressions and gestures. Notice how your teachers move their faces and hands. These will flow in congruence with their paralanguage and eye contact. Their faces may not give too much away (so you have to read their eyes) but their hands will be raised and active when they're talking about topics that engage them.

Questioning your former knowledge

As you review your course notes, question your former knowledge on the topic. Begin to think about everything you already know about the topic and everything you believe will be important for the exam.

Your brain can't comprehend something it doesn't recognize. It works by making associations with knowledge you formed in the past (even if it's wrong). After you've formed ideas about the information you think you'll be tested on (adding to your former knowledge), when you begin to review your course material, what you see as you turn the pages will be associated with knowledge you've previously deemed to be important. Everything you survey that *matches* what you believe is important will become significant. The information jumps out at you. Everything that doesn't match, you'll pass by. This is what your brain (refer to Chapters 2 and 5) is designed to do. It screens out everything that has no personal value to you right now.

Questioning your former knowledge on course content is also useful when the time comes to review your notes properly, because the associations built between the old learning and your study notes strengthens your ability to retain and recall information later.

Finding Additional Information

You've probably got required reading, such as selected articles and text books. You can use a number of techniques to increase your efficiency when reading these, and I show you how to improve your reading techniques in Chapter 9. However, sometimes, you may also be asked to find extra information from books and articles that aren't in your required reading. Finding this information can be time-consuming.

The following steps offer a practical way to make the best use of your time when searching through unfamiliar books in a library:

1. **Question your selection. Ask yourself why you're pulling this particular book off the shelf.**

   Why did you choose this book and not another? What specifically are you looking for? How can this book add more information to support the material you need to prepare for an exam?

   The answers to these questions help you formulate ideas about the specific information you need. After you know what you're looking for, you'll be able to notice anything that matches your ideas.

2. **Be curious about the book you're holding.**

   A sense of intrigue increases your motivation (and speed of reviewing), and helps to build neural connections to your former knowledge.

3. **Skim through the book for 60 seconds to assess its content.**

   Look at the front and back covers, then open the book and read the table of contents. Do any chapter headings hold the information you require? If so, go to Step 4.

   If you're uncertain about the book's value, go to the index (if the book has one) and skim the listings. An index can tell you if the book offers useful information. However, if you can't find a match in the index, put the book back and find another one, going back to Step 1.

4. **Find the chapter you're curious about, and read its introduction and conclusion.**

   The minute or two you spend doing this should be long enough to tell you whether the book will be useful to you.

After you locate the extra books you need, organize them into subject-specific piles in your study space. At this stage, you're simply compiling the books (or information) you need, and determining that you've got the right material. (Reading comes later, and I show you how to review the material while simultaneously looking for ways to condense it into key points in Chapter 9.)

If you want to go to the next stage immediately, browse the contents and index in a book and mark the appropriate pages with a slip of paper or sticky note. This will save a little time later.

Chapter 9

Improving Your Reading Techniques

Many people — even those who like to read — find reading to study tiring. Regardless, you can use many types of styles or techniques to read material, each designed for different purposes.

In this chapter, I explore the different reading techniques you can use to review for exams. The key is to know what your purpose is and then employ the appropriate technique.

I show you how to skim read, study read, and speed read. I also introduce you to a revolutionary way of reading that enables you to absorb an incredible amount of information in a second — photoreading.

Reading for Different Purposes

First of all, you need to determine your purpose when reading any particular book, article, or essay. Do you want to gain a brief general overview of the subject? Do you want to come away with an in-depth comprehensive understanding? Perhaps you just want to relax and read for fun? After you identify your purpose, you can choose from one of the different reading techniques I outline in the following sections.

Deciding on your purpose when reading helps improve your mental focus. You set your intention and direct your brain to read more efficiently. For example, if you have set a clear intention to skim read a chapter, you are less likely to be caught up in the really interesting (but time-consuming), paragraphs that make up the general content of the book.

Don't skip setting your intention. When you don't define your purpose for reading or set your intention to determine what you want to get out of the material you're about to read, your effort may be fruitless.

Seeing in white and black

Take a look at the image shown here. What do you see? Some black shapes? Do you see a word? If not, look at the space between the black shapes.

You've been so conditioned to read black letters on a white background that when you see letters on a black background, it's really hard for your brain to make out the words. Notice, I said, "your brain" because you don't read the words with your eyes, you read them with your brain. Your brain learned to read when you were very young, and possibly the reading habits you use now as an adult are those that were taught to you when you were little. However, you **can** learn to deliberately improve your reading abilities.

By the way, the word in the figure is LEFT. Do you see it now?

Dipping into Your Text: Skim Reading

After you survey a book and decide that it has the information you need, you then need to explore the content. *Skim reading* involves turning to the relevant chapter and reading the introduction and the summary. You now have an overview of the information you're after. If you need to go further, go through the chapter, reading all the main headings, the *topic sentences* (the first sentence in each paragraph), any highlighted key points, plus picture captions, and anything else that stands out on the pages.

Avoid deep reading at this point. The idea behind skim reading is to prime your brain so that you know what's covered in the book. As you see the words, any associated former knowledge in the form of established neural networks start to fire up to make connections.

To practice skim reading, read the article in Figure 9-1. Come back to this page after skimming through the article and write down any key points. You can do so in the margins of this book or on a blank piece of paper.

Digging Deeper into Content: Study Reading

Study reading is the slowest form of reading you'll need to do. The purpose of *study reading* is to absorb what's written so that you retain the information in your long-term memory. If the material doesn't need to be remembered, though (for example, when reading a novel) a speed-reading technique may suffice. I cover speed reading later in this chapter.

In order to get the most out of your study reading time, check out the guidelines and tips in the next sections.

Leading From the Inside
by Ian Richards

Apparently, there are well over two thousand books published each year with the word 'leadership' somewhere in the title. Whether this represents a powerful resource for leaders or an ever-increasing source of yet more confusion is perhaps a matter for debate, but I can't help thinking that there's a need to de-mystify 'leadership' and return to some fundamentals.

Internal and external leadership
One useful and straightforward model involves a theoretical distinction between internal and external leadership, which creates a distinction between our leadership of our 'self' and our leadership of others. Despite its obvious simplicity, there are some sound benefits to this model. Firstly, it provides a tangible rational for that overused phrase 'everyone is a leader', based on the assertion that we all need to 'lead' our own lives even if we manage to convince ourselves that we don't lead or aren't capable of leading others.

That doesn't mean leading your own life is easy. In fact, from my experience, internal leadership is a serious area of weakness for many people and, as will become apparent, it's also a major underlying cause of poor external leadership.

Secondly, the model directs leaders to examine their personal effectiveness in terms of their own lives, their own goals and their own thinking.

Active personal development
To be an effective internal leader you need to be able to examine beliefs, habits and attitudes in order to make constructive adjustments at a subconscious *level* and therefore create new natural or 'free-flow' behaviours. Aspects such as your self-image, self-efficacy, self-esteem and internal accountability need to be developed proactively. This can be very challenging for many people and it never ceases to shock me how many business leaders — many holding formal positions of leadership — have no direction in their own lives and, equally worrying, don't have the required up-to-date knowledge and tools to develop their internal skills.

Open to influence
A lack of internal leadership leaves people open to influence — they follow fashions and trends, believe what experts tell them and perceive their lives as a never-ending stream of things to do. Indeed, their most important targets are merely the next things they perceive they have to do. Without clear direction, priority, balance and cohesion, life for them is stressful beyond measure.

Figure 9-1: A skim reading exercise *(continued opposite).*

This is the organisational leader with the never-ending 'to do' list, the child that is 'easily led', the woman who stays with the abusive partner, the unemployed man who can't see himself in work — no direction, no vision, no internal leadership.

Constructing a personal vision

When people start to construct their own personal vision and develop the skills they need to achieve their goals, they realise they're unable to change and move forward without impacting on, or being impacted upon, others. Here, I would claim that 'impacting on others' often comes in the form of 'influence' which, at the very least, could be described as accidental external leadership. Therefore, 'deliberate influencing' isn't only an accomplished form of external leadership, but it also demonstrates the importance of being in control of the influence you have on others.

Returning to the personal vision, it's clear that, to achieve what they want, the individual needs to engage in activity that brings others on board with their vision and connects them with people who can help them get there. Or, in other words, developing a degree of synchronisation between their vision and the personal goals of those involved in achieving it is key to them achieving what they want. But, hang on, this is now looking very much like external leadership and, of course, that's the point.

External leaders need to create a vision based on an outcome that's real and perceivable to those involved in moving towards it. Crucially, this vision needs to be in sync with some key elements of the leader's own personal aspirations and direction. If it isn't, then they're just pretending and that's hard work.

Aligning personal and professional goals

Failing to synchronise personal and professional goals is what drives leaders crazy and brings out the worst in employees — they won't believe you and they won't believe in you. Leaders also need to work with the stakeholders to build synchronisation between the organisational vision and the personal goals of those individuals. Then your people will want to come to work and contribute to the organisational vision because it helps them work towards achieving their own personal goals.

Getting ready to do study reading

Never open a book and start reading every word from the first page. Always survey the contents of the book to get a general gist of what it covers, then identify areas that are of particular importance. This process should take you about ten minutes, depending on the size and detail of the book.

Start by reading the titles, and drawing on your prior knowledge to prime your brain to build mental associations. Remember, your brain can't comprehend something it doesn't recognize. Scanning a book (refer to Chapter 8) and skim reading (see the preceding section) create recognition.

If you haven't already done so, read the table of contents to summarize the main points that you're about to read (refer to Chapter 8 for more on this point). Each chapter in the book may have an outline, discussed in the introduction or summary. Read this and allow yourself a moment to let the material sink in.

The process of mental development, or *incubation*, is important because it gives your brain time to form neural pathways. This is a key reason why going straight into study reading for comprehension without skim reading first can cause mental confusion. Skim read first, question your former knowledge, and gently study read with periods of incubation. This allows your brain to form the strong neural pathways it needs that lead to good memory retention and recall.

Taking in the facts

All study reading should be approached with ease (without tension). Relax and breathe. Drink some water. Read the major headings and then look at the beginning of each paragraph. This is usually the topic sentence and gives an insight into what's covered in the following paragraph. You can get a good understanding of each paragraph by just reading the first sentence in each one. However, if you need more comprehension, read the entire paragraph.

Work your way through the chapter, reading from beginning to end. Make a mental note of any illustrations, lists, and graphs. After you've reviewed and read the main points in each chapter, write down keywords or draw a diagram or concept map (see Chapter 10) to summarize what the chapter is about.

Ask yourself questions and give yourself answers about the text as you draw your diagram. This helps consolidate your understanding of the material. It also helps you to retain the information in your long-term memory.

Going over class notes

As you study read your class notes, look for keywords in each paragraph that represent that entire chunk of information. The idea is to look for ways to condense your linear class notes into visual formats. You want to choose keywords that will bring an entire paragraph to the forefront of your brain when you recall that one word.

Comprehension quiz

One way to check how much information you retain when study reading is to take the following quiz that asks questions about the article in Figure 9-1. Grab a piece of blank paper and write down as many answers as you can from memory. Then check your answers against mine, listed upside down at the bottom of the quiz. Although you may not answer questions exactly as I do, you can count something similar as a correct answer.

1. In this article, the author offers two types of leadership. What are they called?

2. Good internal leadership primarily involves what?

3. What is the prerequisite for good external leadership?

4. What problems do externally orientated leaders have if they haven't developed internal leadership?

5. Approximately how many books are published each year with "leadership" in the title?

6. What core skills make an effective internal leader?

7. What is one key step to developing internal leadership?

8. What is one effective way mentioned to get others on board with your vision?

Answers:

1. Internal and external leadership. 2. An understanding of one's own self. 3. Good internal leadership — as external flows on from internal leadership. 4. Find it hard to motivate themselves or others to any greater vision or higher performance. 5. 2,000. 6. Someone who is able to consistently examine attitudes, beliefs, and habits that might be hindering themselves and others. 7. Developing a personal vision and acquiring the knowledge and skills needed to achieve it. 8. Discover the personal and professional goals of all involved and see if these can be aligned with the greater vision for the group.

Testing your comprehension

Testing your comprehension after you study read is useful to discover how much information has sunk in. One way to test your retention is to team up with a friend and try to explain to her what you've learned. Your friend could also ask you questions about the content you've read.

In "Dipping into Your Text: Skim Reading" earlier in this chapter, I suggest that you read the article in Figure 9-1. This time around, I want you to read the same article, and test how well you're study reading for comprehension. When you've finished reading the article, quickly jot down in diagram form the key points that stood out for you.

Going Faster: Speed Reading

In the interest of saving time when you read, you can often use speed reading.

Speed reading requires you to move your eyes across a page of text in a unique way — usually different from the way you originally learned to read. Like me, you probably began by first learning individual letters, then sounding out your words by their syllables, then saying whole words by themselves, using your finger to guide you across the page, word by word. Now this reading style is a habit.

Speed reading takes the process another step, and involves reading groups of words at once and still understanding the content.

To train yourself to speed read, relax into alpha state (refer to Chapter 5), then place a book in front of your eyes. What you're aiming to achieve is to train your eyes to stop looking at each individual word and focus on whole lines at a time. Stop only three times along each line: At the left third of the line, then the middle third, then the right third.

When speed reading, try not to say the words to yourself as you read. This only slows you down. As you get more skilled at speed reading, see if you can read and understand the text without an inner dialogue.

Reading with speed

Have a go at reading the following paragraph. Because this is a narrow passage, you need to focus your eyes only on the two halves of the text either side of the break point.

Speed reading enables you to take in whole lines of information quickly. If the page is narrow, you would stop your eyes only twice across each line, like this. If it is a wide page, you might need to stop three times to read each third.

How did it go? Were you able to see the groups of words at one time? Were you able to see them without vocalizing them in your mind? This is an example of the kind of skills you can learn to develop through speed reading.

You may speed read at times without knowing that you're doing it. For example, if you were reading a newspaper or magazine with short lines (that is, the content is arranged in columns), your eyes would only look at the left half, then the right half of each line. That's speed reading at its most basic.

It takes time to increase the periphery of your focal point to see groups of words at once, while simultaneously being aware of not vocalizing in your mind. It is a useful skill to develop and one that will save you time in the long run.

When you start practicing speed reading in earnest (particularly with books), don't be too worried if you don't understand the information very well. At this stage you want to focus on creating a new habit — moving your eyes differently. Soon the method will become an automatic way of reading — you won't have to consciously think about moving your eyes differently, and you'll be able to turn your attention to comprehending what you read.

To discover more about speed reading, check out TurboRead Speed Reading at www.turboread.com. This website offers general information about reading and online tests to check your reading speed.

Going beyond Speed Reading: Photoreading

A few years ago, a new method of reading became available following a breakthrough in understanding the way people's brains read and process information. Called *photoreading*, this style of reading bypasses your conscious, analytical mind to use your other-than-conscious mind to absorb text on a page at approximately 25,000 words a minute. The method was developed by Paul Scheele and his colleagues at the Learning Strategies Corporation in the United States.

Scheele believes that the human eye can take in ten million bits of information a second, which means your brain can nonconsciously register an entire page of information like a photograph as you rapidly turn the pages of a book — if you train it to do so. The trick is to trust that this information is going in and then to use another process to bring it into your conscious mind.

Comprehension is also retained when photoreading, with people reporting that they're able to write about or converse on a subject they had no previous knowledge of prior to photoreading about it.

For step-by-step information on how to photoread, check out the Learning Strategies website, www.learningstrategies. com/PhotoReading/Home.asp.

Testing your reading speed

If you'd like to see whether your current reading speed is below, above, or about average, read the article in Figure 9-1, using these directions: Time yourself for 60 seconds, reading the article from the first paragraph. Stop reading after 60 seconds. Then locate the 240th word, shown in italics in the fourth paragraph.

You look for the 240th word because the average reading speed is 240 words a minute, and at the end of the test you'll have an idea if you read slower or faster than others.

Chapter 10

Preparing Your Study Notes

. . . .

In This Chapter

▶ Finding keywords in your class notes

▶ Using mind mapping to visually arrange your topic's keywords

▶ Grouping related ideas with concept maps

▶ Creating essay route maps to structure your ideas

▶ Working with different visual formats

. . . .

*W*hether you're at high school, university, or preparing for a career exam, to make the notes you take during class effective study aids, you need to rewrite them. Your notes are generally linear in nature, but your brain thinks in pictures, so knowing how to create keyword pictures and patterns helps you produce effective study materials. Visual formats enable easier memory retention.

In this chapter, I offer you a variety of ways to turn information into visual formats. I show you how to extract keywords from notes, documents, and books, and how to use mind mapping to visually outline your topic. I also show you how to organize related information using concept maps and essay route maps.

Condensing Your Notes

As you review the notes you took during classes and lectures, look at ways to extract keywords that represent larger chunks of information. You can then insert these keywords into a new format that presents the information visually, so that it's easier to remember.

To get started, select course notes that you need to review. Any subject will do. Now, take a moment to relax your body and mind and set your intention. Your purpose is to find keywords that represent a paragraph or a larger selection of ideas. These words will form your new condensed notes for later study and review.

Begin by writing down the main topic from your selected notes. As you review your notes, list the key themes presented and give each one a heading. Then extract keywords for each theme. Try to extract a minimum of four main themes and five keywords on each theme, extracting approximately 20 key words. Finding keywords in your course notes should not take too long — usually no more than five minutes.

You're now ready to present these keywords in a visual format, using one of the mapping techniques I offer in this chapter. (To see how effectively you can apply your keywords to different types of maps, check out "Applying Visual Formats: A Practical Guide" at the end of this chapter.)

Diagramming a Mind Map

Mind mapping is a great way to brainstorm, classify information, or structure ideas, whether you're taking notes, organizing workloads, solving problems, or reviewing study materials for memory retention.

Mind mapping involves creating a tree-like diagram, arranging keywords and pictures around a central topic or idea placed in the middle of a page. You draw your topic's main groups or themes as colored branches, spreading out from the center. You then add keywords and small illustrations to each branch. You can also add more information by including sub-branches attached to each main branch.

Figure 10-1 shows a mind-mapping example that summarizes the information covered in this book. Although I can't show you the colors I used in my map on this black-and-white page, you get the idea.

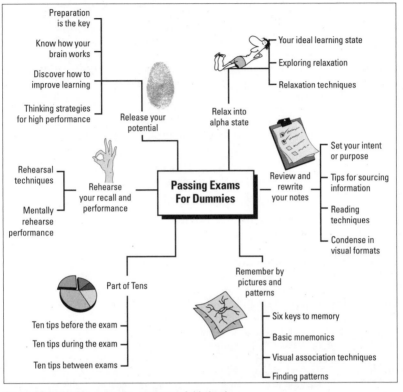

Figure 10-1: Mind mapping the contents of this book.

To begin mind mapping, follow these steps:

1. **Review your notes, identifying the keywords in each main section.**

2. **Write your topic in the middle of a blank page. Then, from memory, jot down the keywords you identified in Step 1, arranging them around the page to summarize the main headings in your notes.**

Working from memory in this step helps you to visualize the key points in your mind — and it's an opportunity to review the main points of the topic.

3. **List the main points of each keyword alongside or below it, grouping related ideas together so that as your eyes follow the map on the page, each branch has its own theme.**

4. **Look at your notes and add more information to the branches (and sub-branches) on your map.**

5. **Make the map as visual as possible, using a different color for each branch and incorporating associated pictures to the main branches. Use arrows to represent relationships between key points.**

6. **Spend time reviewing your map as the exam draws closer.**

For some people, mind mapping is an effective memory aid. For others, mind mapping is a great way to condense large amounts of information to use with other memory techniques. No matter how you use it, mind mapping can be a helpful study aid.

If you want, you can use mind-mapping software to map a topic's keywords instead of drawing your own by hand. Mind Manager, developed by MindJet (go to www.mindjet.com or www.mindsystems.com.au), is one tool you can use to turn your class notes into visual maps. To find other tools, search the Internet for mind mapping software. Some of these tools cost money; others are freeware. Even products you need to pay for generally offer free trial periods. Check out the examples on Illumine Training's website, www.mind-mapping.co.uk/mind-maps-examples.htm to see how creative mind mapping can be. Buzan World, www.buzanworld.com, run by Tony Buzan (who, along with his brother, popularized mind mapping in the 1980s), offers a load of information and resources on mind mapping, designed to improve speed reading and memory retention. You can watch Tony discussing mind mapping on YouTube. Go to www.youtube.com/watch?v=MlabrWv25qQ. Also check out *Mind Mapping For Dummies*.

Connecting Ideas with Concept Maps

Concept maps are simple note-taking formats that enable you to see your linear notes visually. A *concept map* is a diagram that shows a mental model of linear information to help you clarify ideas and concepts.

In a concept map, you condense and organize your ideas by placing keywords in boxes or circles on a page and drawing lines to connect linked words or phrases. Concept mapping techniques vary (and go by different names), but the four main types are the spider map, hierarchy map, flowchart map, and the systems map. I explore each in the following sections.

Concept maps are very flexible, and with a little imagination you can use them to visually represent almost any kind of information. For example, you can use a concept map to illustrate questions that require you to classify information (such as define-and-discuss questions) or to critically evaluate a topic (in cause-and-effect relationship questions). You can also use concept maps to illustrate knowledge, brainstorm, or show problem-solving abilities.

The four basic concept maps I present in this chapter are very easy to draw, or you can use software to create them. Microsoft Word's Diagram Gallery, for example, includes some basic concept mapping tools (although Microsoft uses different names, such as the Radial Diagram tool to create a simple spider map). To use the tools in your Word program, open a document that you want to add a concept map to, and from the main menu select Insert⇨Diagram, then choose the diagram type you want to use. The diagram outline then appears on the page and you simply insert your keywords in the circles or boxes provided. You can also reorganize the diagram's shape, layout, and style, and even add color and make it three dimensional, if you want.

For a more professional approach, use software that creates polished maps. One example is Smart Draw (www.smartdraw.com), which offers a concept mapping tool you can download for free to your computer.

Spreading out a spider map

A *spider map* shows related themes around a main topic and is great for brainstorming. Similar to mind mapping (refer to "Diagramming a Mind Map" earlier in this chapter), in a spider map you write the main topic in the center of the page and create outward branches for each subtopic. You then insert related themes in each outer circle. Spider maps use lines and words in circles — mind maps just use lines — but essentially they achieve the same purpose.

Figure 10-2 shows the format of a basic spider map with keywords placed around a central theme. You can also add notes on each branch if you're drawing your spider map by hand.

Placing two spider maps side by side enables you to make comparisons between two related subjects — for example, to organize key information for a compare-and-contrast essay question. You can quickly produce two spider maps on a sheet of paper using the keywords you extract from your notes. Write the two topics you're comparing in the two main center circles, as shown in Figure 10-3. Then write the contrasting points in the outer circles, and in the inner circles write the comparable points.

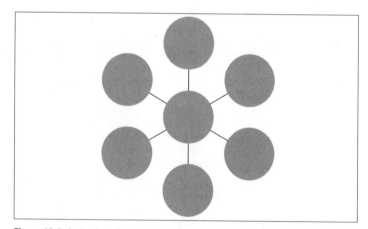

Figure 10-2: A simple spider map, with circles placed around a central circle.

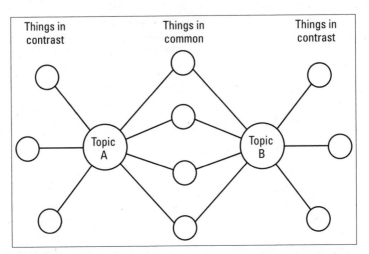

Figure 10-3: A spider map showing how to group key points when comparing and contrasting information for an essay.

Ranking information with a hierarchy map

A *hierarchy map* organizes information in a descending order of importance from the top down, as shown in Figure 10-4. Hierarchy maps are helpful when you need to condense and organize large amounts of information into keywords, below a central topic (for example, if you're studying for exams on science or social studies topics).

Write your topic in the top box and the subcategories in the boxes on the next level. Then write specific keywords under each subcategory. For example, if you were studying attachment theory for a human development exam, write Attachment Theory in the top box. Next, put the theorists (such as Bowlby, Ainsworth, and Karen) in the next level, followed by each of their theory's keywords in the boxes under their names.

Visually representing your linear class notes this way allows you to recall information far more easily than trying to memorize lines on a page.

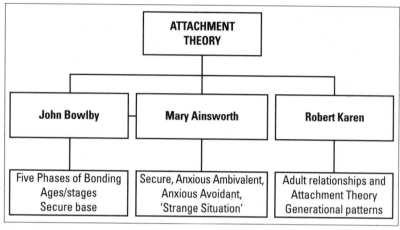

Figure 10-4: A hierarchy map.

Organizing a flowchart

A *flowchart* (see Figure 10-5) is a common mapping tool used to show ideas in a linear format. Technical manuals often use flowcharts to show troubleshooting scenarios.

Flowcharts help identify the relationships between the sections and subsections of a topic (by order of numbers, operations, steps, and so on). They also help you order information into a logical sequence. Similar to essay route mapping (see "Planning Literary Pathways: Essay Route Maps" later in this chapter), you can use a flowchart to sequence ideas for an essay from introduction to conclusion.

In the main left-hand box, write the topic name. In the central boxes, list your keywords in sequence, from the top down (with Introduction in the top box and Conclusion in the bottom box). Add boxes on the right-hand side to list extra information relating to specific keywords.

You can turn information you present in a hierarchy map (refer to the preceding section) into a flowchart to condense a simple essay plan. Doing so helps you to sequence the relevant information in logical order.

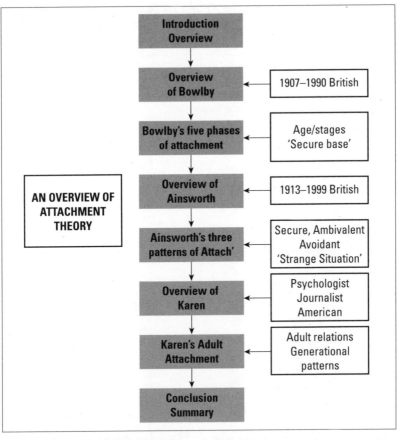

Figure 10-5: A flowchart concept map.

Circling around a systems map

A *systems map* is similar to a flowchart but emphasizes a system's inputs and outputs. These inputs and outputs are the causes and effects influencing how the system operates and organizes itself.

You can apply systems maps to illustrate many different topics. For example, in biology, you can use a systems map to illustrate the different facets of the digestive system. In history, you can use a systems map to show the rise and fall of an empire, and highlight when dominant leaders entered and exited the political scene. In geography, you can use a system map to show the influences and effects of humans in a region.

To draw a systems map, you simply write the inputs and outputs in the left- and right-hand arrows, then add your keywords — the factors that influence the systems — between the circular arrows. Figure 10-6 is a template for a systems map.

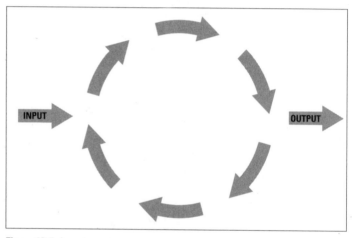

Figure 10-6: A systems map.

Planning Literary Pathways: Essay Route Maps

Essay route maps can help you plan and write essays for assignments and exams. You can use them to help you organize an essay in sequence, mapping out a visual route that states exactly what information fits where, paragraph by paragraph, from the introduction through to the conclusion. This is an extremely helpful note-taking technique if you need to collect and synthesize ideas and information for your essay from many different sources. This is typical of university-level essays, but equally applicable to high school essays as well.

The essay question determines how many sections your essay route map needs. Plan your essay outline, deciding what information will go in each main section, as defined by your essay question. As you source information on each section, make location notes to remind you where to find that great quote or idea you want to use. You can also tag book pages with the route map's section number.

Get an example or two of an exam essay question that's likely to be asked, so you can prepare an essay route map that has broad information you can adapt to suit any related exam question.

Many high school exam essays involve analyzing and writing about different aspects of a book studied during the year. Figure 10-7 shows an example of a handwritten essay route map that explores the characterization of the Shakespeare play *Othello*. Here, a student has decided to illustrate Othello's character under four headings using a pattern of words that start with *D* — Devoted, Deception, Doubt, and Death.

Notice how starting from the top, at the Introduction, the main headings are listed as numbered lines extending right and left from a center line. The subheadings are also numbered. The keywords are placed under each subheading and the source of the information is noted. Location notes are placed in the route map (and on the document) to show you where to find it again when you're ready to write the essay.

After you organize all the keywords and location notes for all the subheadings, you can write the essay in full. The final step is to take the prepared essay content and memorize it for the exam, which I show you how to do in Chapter 13.

Figure 10-8 shows an essay route map prepared for a university essay on human development, called *Attachment and Loss*. Notice how the map logically organizes information from a variety of different sources.

These instructions provide a basic outline on how to create essay route maps. For more detailed information, check out the essay route map resources on my website at www. passingexams.co.nz.

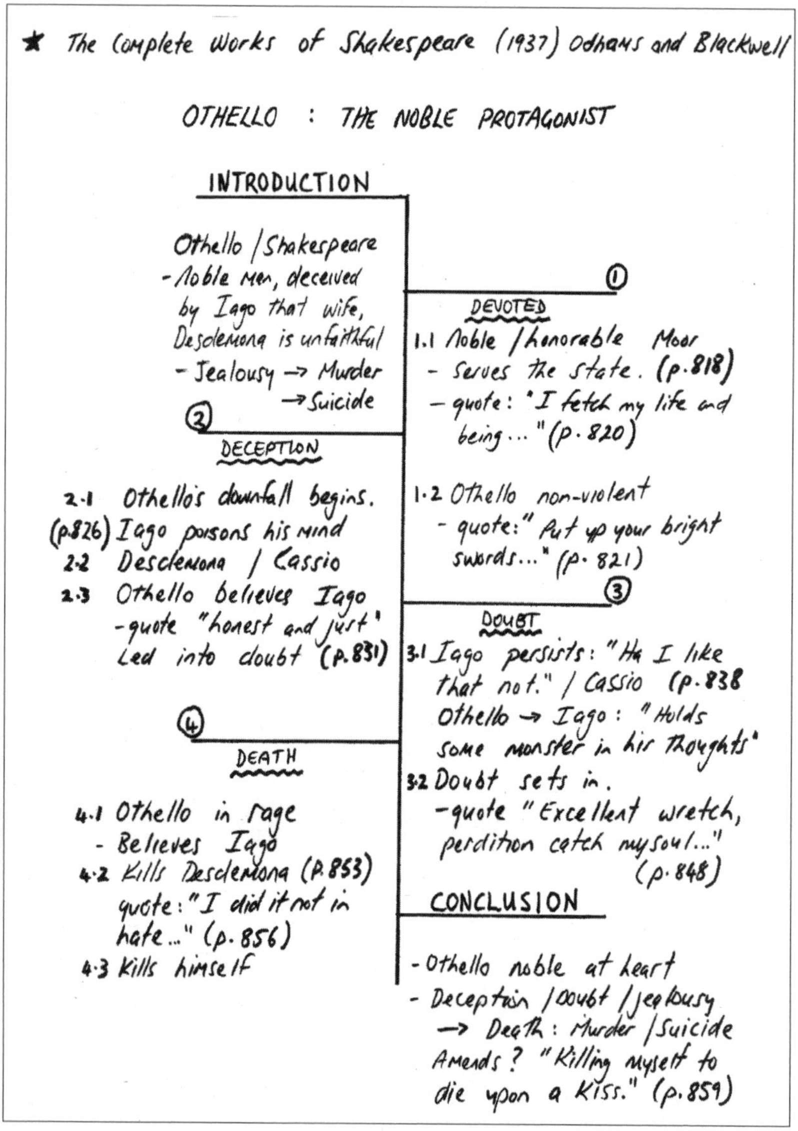

★ The Complete Works of Shakespeare (1937) Odhams and Blackwell

OTHELLO : THE NOBLE PROTAGONIST

INTRODUCTION

Othello / Shakespeare
- Noble Men, deceived
by Iago that wife,
Desdemona is unfaithful
- Jealousy → Murder
→ Suicide

② DECEPTION

2·1 Othello's downfall begins.
(p.826) Iago poisons his mind
2·2 Desdemona / Cassio
2·3 Othello believes Iago
- quote "honest and just"
Led into doubt (p.831)

④ DEATH

4·1 Othello in rage
- Believes Iago
4·2 Kills Desdemona (p.853)
quote: "I did it not in
hate..." (p.856)
4·3 Kills himself

① DEVOTED

1·1 Noble / honorable Moor
- serves the state. (p.818)
- quote: "I fetch my life and
being..." (p.820)

1·2 Othello non-violent
- quote:" Put up your bright
swords..." (p.821)

③ DOUBT

3·1 Iago persists: "Ha I like
that not." / Cassio (p.838
Othello → Iago : "Holds
some monster in his Thoughts"
3·2 Doubt sets in.
- quote "Excellent wretch,
perdition catch my soul..."
(p.848)

CONCLUSION

- Othello noble at heart
- Deception / doubt / jealousy
→ Death: Murder / Suicide
Amends? "Killing myself to
die upon a Kiss." (p.859)

Figure 10-7: A handwritten essay route map showing the arrangement of keywords for ideas and quotes from a Shakespeare play.

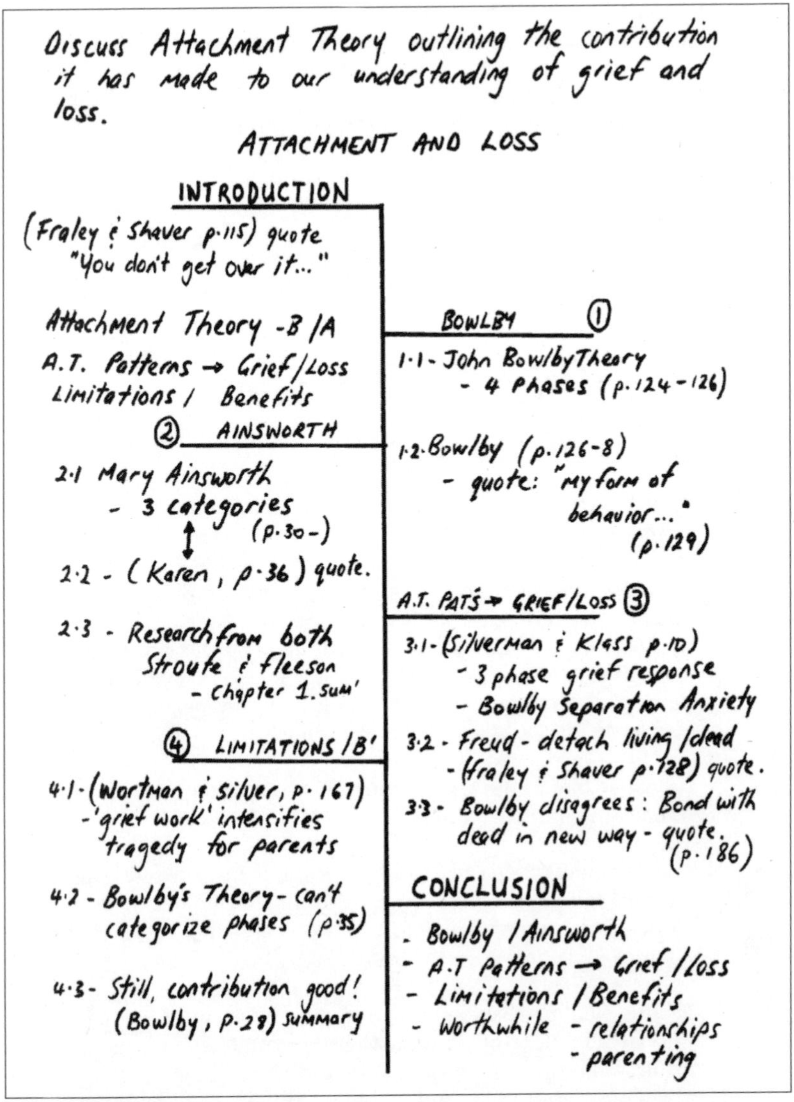

Discuss Attachment Theory outlining the contribution it has made to our understanding of grief and loss.

ATTACHMENT AND LOSS

INTRODUCTION

(Fraley & shaver p.115) quote
"You don't get over it..."

Attachment Theory - B/A
A.T. Patterns → Grief/Loss
Limitations / Benefits

② ___ AINSWORTH

2.1 Mary Ainsworth
- 3 categories
↕ (p.30-)
2.2 - (Karen, p.36) quote.

2.3 - Research from both
Stroufe & fleeson
- chapter 1. sum'

④ LIMITATIONS /B'

4.1 - (Wortman & silver, p.167)
- 'grief work' intensifies
tragedy for parents

4.2 - Bowlby's Theory - can't
categorize phases (p.35)

4.3 - Still, contribution good!
(Bowlby, p.28) summary

BOWLBY ①
1.1 - John Bowlby Theory
- 4 phases (p.124-126)

1.2 Bowlby (p.126-8)
- quote: "my form of
behavior..."
(p.129)

A.T. PAT'S → GRIEF/LOSS ③

3.1 - (Silverman & Klass p.10)
- 3 phase grief response
- Bowlby Separation Anxiety

3.2 - Freud - detach living /dead
- (fraley & shaver p.128) quote.

3.3 - Bowlby disagrees: Bond with
dead in new way - quote.
(p.186)

CONCLUSION

- Bowlby / Ainsworth
- A.T Patterns → Grief /Loss
- Limitations / Benefits
- Worthwhile - relationships
- parenting

Figure 10-8: A handwritten college-level essay route map showing the arrangement of keywords for ideas and quotes from a variety of different sources.

One of the biggest problems students have when writing essays is finding a way to organize the masses of potential content they have. They often ask, "From the books, journal articles, and Internet documents I found, which information should I select, and where exactly is the best place to put it after I do select it?" I had the same problem when I was a student learning to write essays. To solve this problem, I began creating essay route maps and found the method so effective that one year, I scored at the top of my class in three subjects. All the assignments were essays, as were the exams. The university gave me an award for excellence — proof that the technique works!

Applying Visual Formats: A Practical Guide

In this section I summarize ways you can use different visual formats.

First, take the selection of 20 keywords you extracted from your course notes in the "Condensing Your Notes" section at the beginning of this chapter and think about how to convey this information using mind mapping. Take a piece of blank paper and arrange your keywords around the page, writing the keywords for separate branches in different colors.

Next, use one of the concept map formats to outline one of the themes in your class notes.

Concept maps help you classify questions or critically evaluate a topic. You can also use them for brainstorming, illustrating knowledge, problem-solving, and showing higher-order thinking abilities.

Finally, plan an essay assignment using an essay route map. Choose a book or other topic that you could also use in an exam. Analyze the essay question to determine the number of sections your essay route map needs. Name and number these sections and then decide what you could discuss in each section. Number the subheadings. Now that you know what you're looking for, choose the information to go under each subheading. Write in your keywords, quotes, and source notes. Then, mark the source materials with the route map section headings. Well done!

Part IV
Remembering with Pictures and Patterns

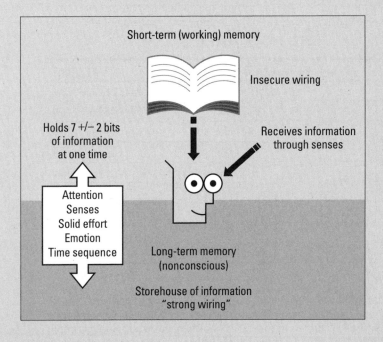

Short-term (working) memory

Insecure wiring

Holds 7 +/− 2 bits
of information
at one time

Receives information
through senses

Attention
Senses
Solid effort
Emotion
Time sequence

Long-term memory
(nonconscious)

Storehouse of information
"strong wiring"

Visit www.dummies.com/extras/passingexams for
a free article (and link to an audio MP3) about how I used
memory techniques to score A+ grades and an award for
excellence.

In this part . . .

- ✓ Discover the six key principles and everyday techniques to improve memory.

- ✓ Delve into using simple mnemonics to remember keywords that represent larger chunks of information.

- ✓ Try out using picture association to rapidly enhance your memory.

- ✓ Arrange content into patterns that sequence information.

- ✓ Find out how to remember exam essay content for easy recall during an exam.

Chapter 11

Making the Most of Memorizing Skills

Memory works through the process of brain cells (neurons) making connections with each other. The stronger and denser your neural connections, the better your memory. Learning requires memory, and the more you understand how your learning and memory work, the easier you'll be able to implement skills that improve your retention and recall.

In this chapter, I examine six principles that affect how memory works: Intention, pictures, emotion, movement, location, and repetition. When you apply these principles to help retain your class notes, you can make dramatic improvements to your exam performance.

This chapter also includes some ways to test these memory techniques. With a little practice, you can build your confidence in your ability to learn and retain information and your ability to do well on the toughest exams.

Use It or Lose It

Did you learn to play a musical instrument when you were young — the piano or guitar, perhaps? Learning to play music requires you to use your memory, right? You set your goal, focus your attention on the task, practice the placement of your hands on the keys or strings and, pretty soon, you remember what to do the next time and the next, until it's wired in and you can play with very little conscious recall. Playing the piece of music is turned over to your memory, and it flows.

Research into adult learning and memory by Michael Merzenich and colleagues using the neuroplasticity model (refer to Chapter 2 for more information on neuroplasticity and the changeable nature of the human brain), suggests that your thinking brain, the cerebral cortex, is like a living creature with an appetite. You have to feed and exercise your brain to keep it healthy and functioning well. Do this, and your brain will physically rewire itself for any task you want to learn — the piano, guitar, history, calculus, accounting, or whatever. Your brain, in fact, allows you to learn how to learn with every activity you undertake. You use it or lose it, as the saying goes.

If you don't use your brain, connections between brain cells weaken, and your memory along with them. By repeatedly reviewing and rehearsing the material you need to recall in an exam, you "wire" it into your brain and enhance your memory.

Six Keys to Good Memory

By utilizing the six principles I explain in the following list and elaborate on in the following sections — individually or in combination — you can easily improve your retention and recall when preparing for exams:

- ✔ **Intention:** To memorize anything well, you need to set your intention, or purpose, and decide why you want to memorize the information. When you set your intention, you tune your brain's attention, concentration, and motivation to the task (more on each in Chapter 7). These three aspects affect your thinking and are required in order to get the information in.

- ✔ **Pictures:** Memory works best when you use pictures. That's why finding ways to convert linear class notes into visual formats, such as concept maps (refer to Chapter 10), is useful. You're more likely to recall keywords in a picture than from lines on a page.

- ✔ **Emotion:** The more exaggerated, strange, magical, sexy, vulgar, or painful your pictures are, the more likely it is that you'll remember them. Any strong emotion works.

(For information on the link between emotion and memory, refer to Chapter 2.)

✔ **Movement:** Memory works best through association or by making connections. The best way to make connections is to add movement or action to your pictures. A visual story with action is a great way to remember and recall information.

✔ **Location:** If a moving, emotional, visual story begins at a particular location, your memory can find and access the story more easily. The location you create is simply a *memory peg* — a prearranged picture that's already stored in your memory.

✔ **Repetition:** Rehearsing your recall three to seven times in your mind ensures the information is locked in. This rehearsal strengthens the neural wiring and transfers information in short-term memory storage to long-term memory storage.

Focusing on one thing at a time

Setting your intent or purpose to establish why you want to memorize something is a key factor in helping you get the information into your head. (I show you how in Chapter 7.) For one, your attention is focused and not scattered.

Many memory problems are caused when your attention is divided at the point when you're required to remember something.

Multitasking is a good example. Although you think you're being efficient when you multitask, your brain can only consciously attend to one thing at a time. You may believe you're doing several things simultaneously, but your brain is actually doing one task, and the second and third tasks very hurriedly afterwards. Unless a task is to the point where you can do it automatically without thinking about it, trying to do it while doing something else as well only distracts your brain and reduces your attention, concentration, and motivation — all important factors to good memory.

The trick is to practice a task enough so that it can run from your memory, then add a new task to engage your conscious mind. For example, while you're doing the dishes — a routine you've practiced enough that it's embedded in your memory and you do without conscious thought — you can multitask by consciously listening to a recording of your study notes or singing or saying them aloud.

A key way to improve memory is to state your intention and fix your attention on one thing from beginning to end. Focusing enhances your memory.

Using vivid pictures or patterns

Some brain researchers suggest that when you think about something, you don't create pictures in your head so much as a representation of reality developed from vast neural and astrocyte processes. (I explain astrocytes and brain processes in Chapter 2.) For many people, a lot of processing happens in the primary visual cortex of the brain and that is why you can see an image in your mind's eye.

The visual connection explains why memory can be enhanced by converting linear class notes into visual formats (refer to Chapter 10) and, taking this idea one step further, by converting all your keywords, symbols, and numbers from your condensed review notes into pictures as well. If these keyword pictures are then linked together, you can begin to form little visual stories — a memory technique ideally suited to memorizing content for exam essays.

Deliberately finding or constructing patterns in your notes strengthens associations between ideas.

Patterns enable your brain to associate related information to form a concept. As far as your brain is concerned, astrocytes (that make up 76 percent of your brain cells) keep watch over repeated neural sequencing and eventually enable you to predict the information coming through your senses. You "just know" stuff about a concept and can use this understanding in different contexts. This function of your semantic memory explains why patterns help you remember stuff. (Refer to Chapter 4 for more on memory.)

Your brain's ability to associate different concepts is why simple rhymes are effective memory tools. How do you remember the number of days in each month of the year? Perhaps you use a rhyming verse? The rhyme uses sound as the pattern: Thirty days has September, April, June, and November. All the rest have 31, except for February .... You know the rest. (For more information on mnemonics, see Chapter 12.)

Adding emotion

Adding emotion to your pictures helps improve your memory. But if learning and memory work physically through neural links forming associations with each other, why would emotion do anything?

The answer lies in the neurochemical releases that occur when what you're perceiving has a high emotional element. The wiring is routed strongly and astrocytes that only work chemically can pick up the neural sequencing more quickly. This helps upgrade your memory from short term to long term.

Scientists now know that the *nucleus basalis* within the limbic system in your brain plays a role in enhancing memory. This area releases two neurotransmitter chemicals during stimulating learning or study: *Dopamine* gives a pleasurable feeling, acting like a reward for thinking this way; and *acetylcholine* helps focus your attention and, in turn, sharpen your learning and memory.

Picture this

To see how your brain remembers keywords, take a look at the words *yellow, green, red*, and *blue*.

Now, take a moment to think about the word *yellow*. If you were asked to memorize it for an exam, what do you feel naturally drawn to do? Do you think of a yellow object — a yellow flower, for example? If so, your brain has processed *yellow* visually. Or, perhaps you saw the size and shape of the letters in the word itself? Still you thought by imaging.

Try this exercise again on the word *green*. What image construct do you get? Then do the same with *red* and *blue*.

To improve your ability to recall these four colors, try linking your four images together. Add a little action, some emotion, and repeat the sequence a few times. That's it — you've dramatically enhanced a memory.

The trick now is to apply this technique to keywords that matter. Give it a go!

The best way to add emotions to your pictures is to ensure they're strange, unusual, illogical, sexy, rude, or dangerous — any thought that brings forward emotion when you think about it. Finding ways to add emotion to a list of 20 keywords represented in pictures isn't difficult. For example, say you want to memorize fire safety procedures for a firefighters service exam. Fires are dangerous, so you're more likely to remember safety procedures if you build the emotion of fear into the pictures — perhaps your personal safety is in jeopardy as your fire explodes out of control?

Incorporating movement

Brain researchers sometimes say, "Neurons that fire together, wire together." Strengthening the wiring in your brain by firing off many neurons simultaneously strengthens your memory retention and your recall. (I discuss these reactions in the five principles of learning outlined in Chapter 2.)

Ensuring that your pictures provoke an emotional response, coupled with getting them moving or active, fires off more neural activity. Both emotion and movement improve memory.

The best way to incorporate movement is to take your keywords and link them together into a visual story that runs like an inner movie in your mind. The linking of one keyword to the next strengthens the associations between neurons. Those associations that are closely related are more easily remembered. In other words, you can remember stuff that's closely related because your brain, working through association, can link A + B + C + D, and remember the sequence. Conversely, your brain finds it more difficult to jump from A to D if the association between them is too far apart.

Pegging memory into place

Human memory is very much like computer memory in that it helps if you can create a My Documents folder in your head. When you have a place for storing information, your search to recall it is easier because your brain goes directly to the folder.

These folders are really just prepared pictures, called *memory pegs*, you have already memorized and stored. Memory pegs can be a list of random items or a list in sequence, such as rooms in your house or parts of your body. The idea is that you store pictures of your condensed class notes to these peg pictures and through the association or connections between the pictures, your recall is improved.

Using a key to access good memory (using peg lists) is a more advanced mnemonic. I discuss using peg lists in Chapter 13. Peg lists can be likened to the tag words used to locate information in computer memory.

Practicing to strengthen memory

Because repetition helps strengthen the neural pathways in your brain, the last step in the review process involves practicing or rehearsing — both real and imagined. (For more tips on rehearsing, see Chapters 14 and 15.)

Getting information lodged into your memory takes repetition. Human short-term, or working, memory can cope with seven pieces of information plus or minus two pieces at a given time, and retain those pieces of information for about 20 seconds. Figure 11-1 illustrates this process. This is why condensing large amounts of information into a smaller amount of keywords and practicing your recall of them is useful.

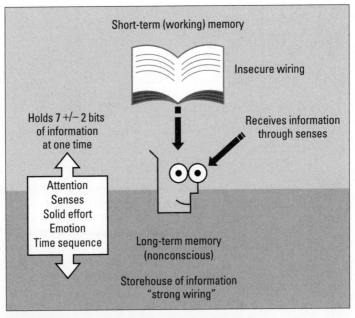

Figure 11-1: How short-term and long-term memory work.

Through repetition, you can transfer and store a vast amount of information into long-term memory. But only repetition will do it — and repetition that uses different sense modalities. Do what you can to ensure you see, hear, and feel the information. Using as many of your senses as possible aids your memory retention, because more neurons and astrocytes are activated at the same time. (See Chapter 2 for more on brain processes.)

The 19th-century memory researcher Hermann Ebbinghaus discovered that the best time to recall (rehearse) information is as soon as possible after it enters short-term memory. He created the *Ebbinghaus curve* (like the one in Figure 11-2) to illustrate that if you don't actively review or practice new information within a short space of time, you forget it.

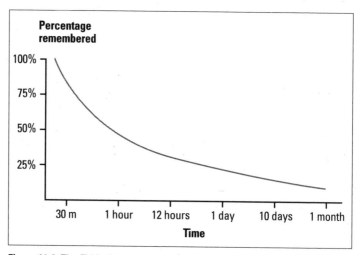

Figure 11-2: The Ebbinghaus curve — recall is dramatically reduced without repetition within 24 hours.

To effectively remember information, review new material as soon as possible — preferably within 24 hours.

Researchers have also discovered that memory seems to be stronger at the beginning and ending of a learning session. This phenomenon is known as the *primacy effect* and *recency effect*. Therefore, as Figure 11-3 shows, it's best to study in short spurts, giving your memory intake many beginnings and endings, as opposed to one large study period that can lead to memory lapses in the middle. Taking short periods for incubation (having lots of rest breaks during a study session) enables the neural wiring in your brain to become more established.

For specific memory tools you can use to enhance your memory, taking into account these factors, see Chapters 14 and 15.

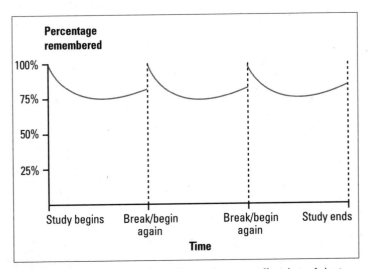

Figure 11-3: Measuring the primacy effect and recency effect. Lots of short review sessions are better than one long one.

Chapter 12

Using Mnemonics: Simple Memory Techniques

*W*hen you understand how memory works (explained in Chapter 11), you can apply different memory techniques to recall condensed review notes quickly.

This chapter offers you a variety of basic *mnemonics* (the first *m* is silent), or memory tools, to help you speed up memory retention. Using any of these simple mnemonics can make a difference to your memory retention and hopefully save you a lot of time avoiding rote (repetitive) memorizing.

Whether you're trying to retain information for a high-school exam, a university exam, or career exam, in this chapter you're likely to discover a technique that suits the way your brain processes and retains information best.

Learning by Rote

The traditional way of enhancing memory involves repetition, and you may find that your default memorizing strategy is to go over and over your notes until you feel you've retained the information. This is called *rote learning* and in some cases it can be effective. For example, you were probably taught to memorize your times tables by rote, practicing them over and over. You can now recall them effortlessly from memory.

Rote learning takes a lot of time. When you're juggling a number of exam subjects or activities apart from reviewing for an exam, you need ways to speed up the retention process.

Memorizing with Mnemonics

Basic *mnemonics* are memory aids that provide a quick and easy way to build retention and recall your information. They work by the association of easily remembered constructs that you can relate back to the information requiring retention. Some of the more common mnemonics include using acronyms and acrostics, maps, music, voice recordings, flashcards, acting, and spreadsheets.

Grouping first letters: Acronyms

Acronyms are one of the most common mnemonic techniques people use to help remember information. An *acronym* takes the first letter from a group of keywords to form another word. For example, the first letters of the North American great lakes — Huron, Ontario, Michigan, Erie, and Superior — spell the word HOMES.

If you need to recall a stack of information on each lake name, you can literally condense all the information into the acronym HOMES so that it becomes easier to remember. To do so, you simply extend the mnemonic with pictures, movement, or emotion (refer to Chapter 11), so that HOMES becomes more meaningful. For example, if you create a picture in your mind, you can visualize your own house floating over five puddles (symbolically representing the five lakes), and as the house dips into each puddle you recall the names: H for Huron, O for Ontario, M for Michigan, and so on.

You can create acronyms in different ways. For example, if you have a number of keywords with the same first letter, you can group them together with a number. For example, the acronym 3M stands for Minnesota Mining and Manufacturing (see the "Common acronyms" sidebar for other examples).

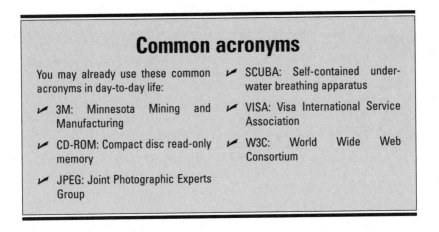

Common acronyms

You may already use these common acronyms in day-to-day life:

- ✔ **3M:** Minnesota Mining and Manufacturing

- ✔ **CD-ROM:** Compact disc read-only memory

- ✔ **JPEG:** Joint Photographic Experts Group

- ✔ **SCUBA:** Self-contained under-water breathing apparatus

- ✔ **VISA:** Visa International Service Association

- ✔ **W3C:** World Wide Web Consortium

You can also make new words by inserting vowels between consonants. For example, if you're memorizing the three key factors in economic theory that influenced people's work and careers — Fordism, Welfarism, and Keynesian Theory —, you can take the F, W, K and insert an 'or' between each letter to make **For WorK**.

You can also use software to create acronyms. Check out AcroMaker at www.acromaker.com or find an alternative tool by typing the words acronym generator into a search engine.

Take a group of keywords from your notes now and practice making an acronym. Whether you're in high school, college, or undertaking a career exam, this simple technique is very effective in helping you to remember facts.

Rhyming with acrostics

Acrostics are similar to acronyms, except they don't try to make a single word. An *acrostic* takes the first letters of a group of keywords to create new words that can be developed into a visual story and in some cases a rhyme. For example, you may have learned an acrostic for remembering the names of the planets in the solar system — Mercury, Venus, Earth, Mars, Jupiter, Saturn, Uranus, and Neptune. The acrostic I learned is: My Very Eager Mother Just Sat Upon Nails.

Acrostics help you to recall the first letters of your keywords, prompting you to remember the whole word. Likewise, you're more likely to remember a group of keyword's first letters if you turn each of them into moving pictures with emotion — in other words, a visual story.

Acrostics are useful for memorizing content and quotes for English essays. For example, to help you memorize a selection of quotes in an exam, select the first letter from each line in the quote to produce a group of letters, then turn each letter into a statement, ditty, or rhyme — your acrostic. Use the acrostic to help you recall all the lines in the quote by simply writing the letters down the margin.

Like a poem, remembering an acrostic can be further enhanced when you rhyme the words or pictures you're using. The rhyme in effect is an *auditory pattern* that enables you to predict, and your memory likes predicting patterns!

Acrostics are also useful in science subjects, which usually require you to memorize a lot of technical information. For example, if you're studying biology, you may need to know the names given to different parts of the brain's neurology. Write down the keywords, as shown in Figure 12-1, then create an acrostic from the first letters. You can then make a strange picture for each letter, and link the pictures into an active and emotional visual story.

Myelin, Dendrite, Neurotransmitter, Fascicle,
Cell Body, Synapse, Axon

My Dentist kNew Fast Cell's Sinful Action

A picture of my dentist and a patient named 'Cell'
(short for Celia), who made inappropriate gestures and
sounds when being treated.

Figure 12-1: Turning an acrostic into a visual story.

Creating rhymes

Make little rhyming slogans to remember information — for example, history teachers in the English-speaking Americas use the rhyme, "In fourteen hundred ninety-two, Columbus sailed the ocean blue."

It's easy to make your own rhymes. And the more strange and unusual they are, the more likely you are to remember them.

Remembering with maps

If you consider yourself to be a highly visual person who sees pictures in your mind's eye really easily, you may find that you can easily memorize visually formatted notes simply by looking at them repeatedly.

The first step is to convert your linear class notes into a visual format, by mind mapping or creating concept maps or essay route maps (I describe how to use these mapping techniques in Chapter 10). After you turn your notes into a visual format, practice writing out your maps from memory. Through repetition, you'll transfer them from short-term into long-term memory in no time.

Using music for memory

You have probably noticed that when you hear a piece of music that you used to listen to long ago, it triggers memories associated with what you were doing back then. You recall all sorts of pictures and feelings. This association uses musical/ rhythmic intelligence.

Your body also has a tendency to synchronize with music. When listening to classical baroque, you hear the music at 56 to 64 beats per minute. Your heart rate matches this beat and your body naturally enters alpha state — the relaxed state ideal for learning and memory retention. (For more information on alpha state, refer to Chapter 5.)

Two specific techniques that involve using music for memory retention are called *active concert* and *passive concert*:

- ✔ An *active concert* has baroque music playing in the background while someone actively reads out loud the text you're learning. You focus on the person's words and allow the music to relax you.

- ✔ In a *passive concert*, you sit in a relaxed position with your eyes closed, focusing on the music while the text is spoken softly beneath it. The music carries the information into your memory more easily because you're in a relaxed state.

Try recording your own active concert or passive concert and play it back over and over, preferably when you're about to sleep or when you awake in the morning. Of course, you can also listen to the recording in the car on your way to school, university, or work — but don't close your eyes!

Making voice recordings

If you know that your brain processes information dominantly through the auditory channel (refer to Chapter 3), a good way to get your condensed notes into memory is to create an audio recording. Try reciting your notes aloud, recording your voice on an audio player, and then, as you get closer to your exam date, listen to your spoken notes as often as possible.

Creating flashcards

Putting your keywords onto small blank cards with the condensed information on the back is another simple memory-rehearsal technique. Drawing on the repetition principle of memory, you look at the keyword and recall the associated information before turning the flashcard over to check you got it right.

Work through the flashcards one at a time, placing those you didn't get correct on a separate pile. Come back to this pile when you've finished the first run-through. Through trial and error, in a short time, you'll pass the correct information into your long-term memory.

Flashcards are a great kinesthetic (physical) approach to recalling or rehearsing information because the cards are a practical means of getting you feeling and moving about, rehearsing as you say aloud the answers to the keywords on the cards.

You can make your own flashcards online. Take a look at this great website: www.flashcardmachine.com.

To speed things up, try making a viewing device by cutting the bottom out of a small box, putting slits in the sides and passing your flashcards through the slits, from one side to the other, one at a time. Try to recall the information as the card comes into view through the bottom of the box. It sounds silly, but this helps enhance your brain's neural processing. Perhaps you can invent other kinesthetic ways to demonstrate your class or review notes.

You can also color code your cards by subject to enhance your visual neural processing. For example, if you need to memorize key information on the terms for the Treaty of Versailles at the end of World War I, you could make five yellow flash cards, each with a keyword on one side outlining each treaty term, and extra information on the opposite side. This mini table shows the information you can write on your yellow flashcards for this subject. The next subject could have red flashcards; the next, blue; the next, green, and so on.

Flashcard key word	*Extra information (on the back)*
War guilt	Germany must accept blame for starting the war.
Reparations	Pay €11.3 billion.
Territories and colonies	Alsace-Lorraine. Polish Corridor. Saarland. No overseas empire. Anschluss forbidden.
Armed forces	100,000 men. Conscription banned. No armored vehicles, six battleships. Rhineland demilitarized.
League of Nations	International police force. Germany not invited.

Acting out

Another kinesthetic mnemonic that aids memory retention is acting. Recite what you're studying out loud, exploring your notes through movement and feeling by using your arms and hands in creative ways in the space in front of you. Pretend you're teaching your topic to an imaginary class.

The information becomes associated not only in your brain but also in your whole body.

You can easily act out any subject you're learning — like the Treaty of Versailles I mention in the preceding section. You don't necessarily need to use flashcards, though. Simply reading from a concept map can prompt your memory as you move around explaining the material. Try this alone or with some friends. You may actually find it fun, and fun releases happy neurochemicals, also helpful for memory retention.

Using spreadsheets

Discovering that placing keywords in a spreadsheet enhances memory may surprise you — as it did me. The reason it surprised me was because it's incredibly effective.

Because my learning and thinking styles are quite logical, analytical, and sequential (refer to Chapter 3 to see how you learn best), I decided to insert an entire year's review notes into the rows and columns of a spreadsheet. Through a mix of acrostics and repetition, I memorized the vertical and horizontal patterns displayed in the spreadsheet and was amazed by the results. I was able to recall everything easily. When it came to the exam, I made sure that each keyword (representing a chunk of information) would cover the exam questions, whether multiple choice, short answer, or essay. The result was an A+, top of the class!

A spreadsheet draws on the pictures/patterns principle of memory. For example, if the very first column in the spreadsheet is five horizontal rows deep, use an acrostic (refer to the section "Rhyming with acrostics" earlier in this chapter) to create a visual story with five keywords. This anchors the information, and forms the peg for each keyword that follows along the rows.

Table 12-1 shows a spreadsheet used to memorize the keywords of the rotational inertia of common shapes for a physics exam. You could use a mnemonic to get your first column down and then, through repetition, memorize each row horizontally, one at a time. The mnemonic in this spreadsheet could then be remembered as a rhyme. Try saying aloud, "HC-2SC-HS-SS," with a rhythmic tone, while clicking your fingers to the beat.

Table 12-1	Spreadsheet for Physics Exam		
Mnemonic Acrostic	*Shape*	*Rotation Angle*	*Formula*
HC	Hollow cylinder	An axis along the center	$I = mr^2$
SC	Solid cylinder (a solid wheel, for example)	An axis along the center	$I = 1/2\ mr^2$
SC	Solid cylinder (a thin rod, for example)	Its end point	$I = 1/3\ mr^2$
HS	Hollow sphere	An axis through its center	$I = 2/3\ mr^2$
SS	Solid sphere	An axis through its center	$I = 2/5\ mr^2$

Chapter 13

Fine-Tuning Your Memory: Advanced Visual Techniques

*R*esearchers have discovered that human memory is enhanced when information is pegged to a specific, physical place. When you create picture pegs (or image tags) in your mind, like a My Documents folder in a computer, your memory can scan its storage and find the information you want. In this chapter, I show you how to use visual association techniques to recall many different types of content. These memory techniques require either a prearranged storage location — simply other image constructs in your mind — or are linked to each other in a chain-like fashion to make a visual story. I provide examples using different content so that you can use these techniques to remember any exam content.

Developing Visual Association Techniques

Visual association techniques extend basic mnemonics by enhancing the way memory can make associations. (Refer to Chapter 12 for information on mnemonics.) This means your information can be connected to prearranged memory-peg pictures, which could be a familiar place (using the location method), or connected to each other (using the story method). I show you how to use these association techniques in the next sections.

Storing pictures by location

The *location method* is a visual association technique that's effective for memorizing collective information. If you need to remember the names of countries around the Mediterranean for a geography or history exam, for example, use the location method to link mental pictures with familiar objects in rooms around your house.

For example, Greece could be visualized as oil on the concrete in your garage; Turkey could be a roast turkey in the fridge in your kitchen; Israel could be a handrail. Get the picture? Now, all you need to do is think of the picture and the country's name will come back to you. The familiar object is the peg that brings the associated information back into your memory.

You may be surprised by your ability to recall information using this method. Take a few minutes to create a picture peg by doing the following exercise:

Close your eyes and think of five rooms in the house where you live. In your mind's eye, see yourself walking through the rooms and noting four objects in each room. Repeat the sequence three times, trying to picture as much detail as possible.

If you can't get pictures in your head, say the names of the objects to yourself as if you're seeing them in your mind. For example, "I'm in the kitchen, there's the sink to my right, plus the oven, fridge, and a fruit bowl."

You can associate picture pegs with keywords you need to remember.

Now, imagine that the following 20 items are keywords related to the content and quotes you've compiled for an essay reviewing a book about a famous sports team:

747	Goal posts	Penalty	Boot
England	Referee	Scrum	Grass
Sports Team	Whistle	Crowd	22
Captain	Line Out	Naked Man	Field
Stadium	Coach	Dog	Try

Because you've already associated four objects in five rooms in your house, you can now assign a group of four keywords to objects in one room. Visualize each word as a strange, illogical, or exaggerated picture in each room of your house. The more unusual you can make your pictures, the better. Funny or exaggerated pictures produce stronger emotions, and emotion strengthens your memory retention and recall. For example:

> A model 747 plane flies through the kitchen's open window and lands in the sink. The Union Jack flag (your picture for England) is draped over the oven. A miniature sports team comes out of the fridge. A man with *Captain* emblazoned on his shirt falls out of the fruit bowl.

You then picture the next room and assign your next four keywords to objects in that room. Continue to associate four keywords with objects until you get through all 20 keywords.

Spend no more than five minutes creating your keyword pictures and pegging them to each room. When you've finished, take out a blank piece of notepaper and try to recall the list by first going to the room in your mind and seeing what pictures you've associated with it.

Linking pictures in your mind

By using your imagination, you can create pictures for all your keywords, then link them to each other (as opposed to associating them with separate picture pegs) to make a visual story. This is called the *story method* and it uses many key components that create strong memories — vivid pictures that are emotional, illogical, and highly active.

The story method is a great technique that can be adapted to fit similar exam essay questions. For example, the story method is easily applied to the example list of 20 items used in the location method in the preceding section.

This time, instead of creating five picture pegs, make one peg — for example, a piece of furniture in your room — as a starting point. Then chain one picture to the next by using your imagination to create a story. If the open window of your kitchen is your peg picture, think of this and then attach your plane coming through.

> The plane lands on the flag which is hanging off the fridge. The plane door opens and all the miniaturized team come skipping out, led by their captain. They all jump into a large tiered wedding cake that represents the stadium with two large candles (goal posts) ... and so on.

Get the story? To use your story to help recall information for an essay in an exam, see "Remembering Exam Essay Content for Easy Recall", later in this chapter.)

Creating a memory peg list

You can take any number of familiar items and turn them into a *memory peg list*. You can create a peg list using the furniture in your house or in rooms at your school or workplace, or you may prefer to use parts of your body instead. Each item is a location where you peg your list.

For example, to create a memory peg list using your body, scan your body in sequence starting at your toes and working your way up to your head — knees, thighs, bottom, stomach, chest, and so on.

If you don't want to use your whole body, try making memory peg pictures using the fingers on your non-writing hand. You can chain complete stories to each finger, giving each one a picture peg. In other words, you could memorize 20 pieces of information and attach it to your thumb picture peg (the thumbs-up gesture). Assign another 20 to your first finger and use the image of you licking that finger as its picture peg, and so on.

The following are sample picture pegs for your entire hand, but feel free to create your own:

- ✔ **Thumb:** Picture the thumbs-up gesture.

- ✔ **First finger:** Picture yourself licking your first finger to turn pages in a book.

- ✔ **Middle finger:** Picture yourself holding a multi-colored pen between your thumb and middle finger as you write furiously.

- ✔ **Ring finger:** Picture a diamond the size of a golf ball on a ring on this finger as you raise your hand to the sky.

- ✔ **Little finger (pinkie):** Picture holding out your little finger and raising it to your lips as if you're talking on an invisible mobile phone.

Now that you have your five picture pegs, what information could you hook to them? You could hook the 20 essay keywords about the sports team (refer to "Storing pictures by location", earlier in this chapter) to one finger:

> You do the thumbs-up gesture towards the sky (using the picture peg for your thumb), just as a miniature plane passes into view. It lands on the flag, which is hanging off the fridge. The plane door opens and the miniaturized team come skipping out, led by their captain...

Now, practice using your first picture peg. As you recall the silly pictures in the story attached to your thumb, write down the associated keywords until you have the entire 20 in front of you.

All this information is attached to your thumb picture peg and you still have another four finger pegs you can use for other information!

Later, when you're sitting in the exam, you simply recall each story by lifting each finger and seeing the first peg picture come to mind. How cool is that?

Creating Symbolic Pictures

Sometimes it's difficult to think of a picture for words you have to memorize. Two ways to deal with this are:

- ✔ Break the word into syllables and try to create pictures of each syllable to chain them together.

- ✔ Use sound-alike pictures or symbolic pictures. These pictures don't have to be a literal translation of the word.

For example, in chemistry, Strontium-90 is a radioisotope used in nuclear power sources. A sound-alike picture could be strong-liam-90 — a muscle-bound, weightlifting 90-year-old with the name *Liam* written above a nuclear power symbol on his shirt.

In the following sections, I include more ways to remember tricky things.

Remembering unusual, foreign, or large words

Have you ever thought about giving foreign-sounding words a meaning so that you can easily remember them? The *substitute-word technique* is an effective way to learn and remember foreign language vocabulary. Take a foreign word — for example, the German word for "paddock" is *Wiese* (pronounced *visa* in English). Obviously, the substitute English word is visa and to remember the word you could simply imagine yourself proudly holding out a large gold Visa card to a real estate agent as you decide to purchase the open paddock in front of you.

Make your word/pictures as ridiculous as possible. The more exaggerated they are, the better chance you have of remembering them.

You can apply the same technique to remember unfamiliar English words. For example, the word *inebriate* means "to make drunk." To remember the word, you could imagine a moldy piece of brie cheese (sounds like ine*brie*ate) in a pub being eaten by a drunken person.

Remembering numbers using visual association

You can remember numbers using pictures as well. You can memorize them using sound-alike images, such as 0 = Hero, 1 = Nun, 2 = Shoe, 3 = Tree, and so on. The other option is to use a symbolic picture. For example, 0 looks like a ring, so you could picture a ring on a finger; 1 looks like a tall tree trunk; and 2 could be a light switch, because a light switch has two settings — on and off.

Take out a blank piece of paper and spend a few minutes making your own pictures for 0 to 9, and then practice recalling the images you assign to the numbers at least three times — that way, you won't forget them.

To remember dates, take the last two numbers and visually chain them together. For example, in European history, the Treaty of Versailles at the end of World War I was signed on the 28th day of June in 1919. To remember this date using your prearranged sound-alike pictures, visually associate them by chaining them together into a story.

First, assign images to the important numbers:

> 2 = shoe, 8 = gate, June = a woman named June,
> 1 = nun, 9 = mine (an explosive).

You don't have to remember the 19 representing the century, just the 19 for the year. Your visual story for this date could be:

> A nun named June (who has her name written on a large name tag on her front) loses her shoe as she climbs over a closed wooden gate with "Versailles" written on the top paling. She gets over the gate and steps on a buried mine. She hears a click, but the mine doesn't go off.

Your story can bring in all the elements you have to remember — Versailles, the war, and the date of the treaty.

Remembering science formulas

You can also remember science formulas and mathematical equations using picture techniques. For example, check out these associations:

- **2b:** Picture two bees flying around.
- **Multiplication symbol ($\times$):** Picture a clock.
- **Square root:** Picture of a large, square tree root.
- **Pie:** Picture of a baked pie.
- **n:** Picture of a hen (sound-alike).
- **Bracket symbol ({}):** A picture of an archery bow (look-alike).
- **1:** Picture of a nun (sound-alike).
- **2:** Picture of a shoe (sound-alike).
- **=:** Picture the sugar substitute Equal.

These symbols, used in equations, can create pictures that, if chained together, can build an interesting visual story. For example, to illustrate sequences in calculus, the notation $\{xn\}$ $n \geq 1$ is used. A visual story could be a large wooden cross (x) with a small hen (n) resting at its base. On either side of the cross are two archery bows: $\{xn\}$. The hen sees another hen that has a small nun (1) riding on its back and tries to knock the nun off with an archery bow: $n \geq 1$.

The more ridiculous your story, the better your chances of recalling it.

Remembering Exam Essay Content for Easy Recall

Not all teachers agree that memorizing essays for exams is a good idea. The main reason is that students who memorize essays may find that the exam question doesn't match what they've memorized.

By combining the story method (explained earlier in this chapter) and essay route mapping (refer to Chapter 10), you can prepare quite specific information that can be used to fit a variety of essay exam questions. This approach is far more efficient and effective than writing out a number of mock essays — the common rote-learning approach.

When you've prepared and written a broad essay outlining what you think can be adapted to suit a variety of similar exam questions, take the keywords from each paragraph and make a new essay route map, writing the keywords in sequence from introduction to conclusion.

For example, imagine that you need to write about Shakespeare's play *Othello*. Figure 13-1 shows the keywords you might use to discuss Othello's character as a noble protagonist.

The next step is to use the story method to memorize the keywords in sequence, visually associating each word/picture from one point to the next and making a silly story from the words. (Note also the 4D-acronym pattern in the introduction that holds the themes of each section of the essay body.) Then with the keywords from the first section, chain them together. Othello (in Noble Service) helps an old dog ("Fetch life ...") and a man (Brabantio) across the road. The man trips over the dog and shouts angrily, but Othello tries to calm him (nonviolent). The man draws his sword, which gleams in the sunlight ("Put up your bright swords ...") and so on.

Practice the sequence of words/pictures aloud three to-seven times to strengthen your neural associations.

Can you see how the story begins to chain all the keyword pictures together? To apply the story method to your essay content, you use your imagination in a different way. Although you may find this hard work to begin with, a little perseverance pays off — you'll find the method easy and save hours of time memorizing essay content by rote.

In the exam, you can quickly draw the essay route map in the space provided for essay planning, and write the keywords to recall your essay plan. You then should be able to write out the essay in full — from memory!

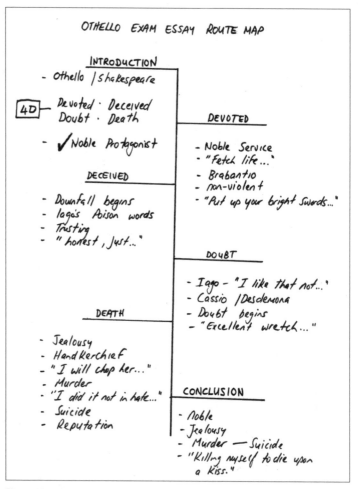

Figure 13-1: A handwritten essay route map for an English exam showing the keywords that can be memorized in sequence using the story method.

Applying Memory-Enhancement Techniques

You need to work out which memorizing techniques work best for you. Trying them out is the best way.

Start practicing mnemonics (covered in Chapter 12) as soon as possible so that you can easily apply the techniques to your subjects' content when exams are approaching. When you start to see the results as you play around with memorizing techniques, your confidence and motivation will improve.

Take out some exam study notes you know you have to memorize for the upcoming exams. Then, with a pen and blank sheet of paper, practice memorizing your information using the techniques outlined in this chapter and in Chapter 12.

After you choose your keywords, use Table 13-1 to select the mnemonics that match your learning style strengths — the way your brain is naturally wired to think (refer to Chapter 3). Try to also use some unfamiliar mnemonics as well, so that you can wire in some new ways for your brain to process information.

Table 13-1	Choosing Mnemonics
Your Primary Learning Style	**Mnemonics to Use**
Visual, verbal	Acronyms
Verbal, auditory	Acrostics
Visual, logical	Maps
Verbal, auditory	Rhymes
Auditory, verbal	Music or voice recordings
Kinesthetic, visual	Flash cards (color-coded)
Kinesthetic, verbal	Acting out
Visual, logical	Spreadsheets

Finally, look back through this chapter for examples of different ways you can peg pictures using the location method, or chain pictures using the story method. These are powerful techniques that really work, but you have to know how to incorporate your content into each or both methods simultaneously. This takes a little time and effort to begin with but when you nail these methods, you'll save yourself lots of time in the long run. Give them a go now!

Part V
Rehearsing for Recall and Performance

Five Strategies to Rehearse for Recall and Performance

- ✔ Practice recalling your information from study notes containing key words extracted from your class notes.

- ✔ Rehearse your recall in ways that use the six principles of memory.

- ✔ Keep the ASSET approach to learning in mind, as you practice recalling your study notes.

- ✔ Write and record a mental rehearsal script to help you visualize your ideal on-the-day exam performance.

- ✔ Don't be afraid to ask for professional help if your exam nerves are getting the better of you.

A strategy to help reduce exam nerves is to mentally rehearse. For a free article (and link to audio MP3) to help you imagine your ideal exam performance, visit www.dummies.com/extras/passingexams.

In this part ...

- ✏ Explore how to recall your study notes in ways that improve your memory.

- ✏ Figure out how to best schedule your time in the days leading up to your exams.

- ✏ Utilize the three Ps (prepare, prioritize, and persevere) to keep you focused.

- ✏ Become familiar with mental rehearsal as a technique to help improve your exam preparation and your performance on the day.

- ✏ Learn about comfort zones and how you can extend them ahead of time to reduce any nerves or anxiety.

Chapter 14

Rehearsing Your Recall

. . . .

In This Chapter

▶ Understanding your learning styles in relation to how you study

▶ Organizing your rehearsal time as the exams get closer

. . . .

*H*ave you ever been in an exam, started answering a question, and then discovered that your mind has gone blank? You know that you reviewed the material, but for some reason the answer just won't come to you.

Getting your condensed review notes (which I talk about in Chapter 10) into your memory is one thing, but getting the information out again is another, especially if you're feeling exam pressure. This is a common occurrence, but you can easily overcome it by practicing your recall before the exam.

When you rehearse your recall of information, you improve your memory. You build confidence in your ability to recollect the information you need during an exam. Similarly, mentally rehearsing being relaxed and confident on exam day imprints your ideal exam situation into your memory. When you come to do it for real, you have stretched your comfort zone ahead of time and are more likely to respond in the way you have imagined.

In this chapter, I cover practicing your recall using the strengths of your preferred learning style. I show you why developing a timetable for rehearsing is important, and how perseverance at this stage of the review process will pay off when you're sitting in that exam room.

Working with Your Learning Styles

Matching memory and recall techniques to your dominant learning styles makes preparing for exams easier.

When you know how your brain prefers to receive, process, and communicate information, you can apply this understanding by using recall techniques that best suit you. (To find out about your learning and thinking styles, take a look at Chapter 3.)

When you're familiar with your learning styles, consider using these techniques to practice your recall for the four styles considered most dominant:

- ✔ **Visual (you learn best by seeing):** Go over color-coded mind maps, concept maps, essay route maps, and other visual notes (pictures/patterns) frequently. (I explain how to compose various maps in Chapter 10.)

- ✔ **Auditory (you learn best by hearing/talking):** Record your notes on an audio device and listen to them often. Reciting notes aloud to others is also helpful.

- ✔ **Kinesthetic (you learn best by feeling and moving about):** Recite your study notes aloud while moving your body as if you're acting them out. Finding physical ways to demonstrate your notes (such as using cue cards) is the key.

- ✔ **Analytical (you learn best by making sense of information):** Think through your notes logically, and practice questions from old exam papers until you understand them. You can also try teaching the material to others.

If you're unsure which learning styles work best for you, try the quick learning style quiz in Appendix C. For more learning styles resources, refer to Chapter 3.

Some brain scientists are not convinced that learning styles are particularly helpful in preparing for exams. However, many believe that if you encourage your brain to process information in many ways (regardless of your learning style preferences) by varying the sense perception channels you receive information through, you can expand your brain's neural networks. Doing so enhances your memory retention and recall, and ultimately improves your exam performance! (See the five principles of learning in Chapter 2.)

The curious case of Rudiger Gamm

Neuroplasticity, or the ability to rewire the brain (covered in Chapter 2), is achievable, and scientists discovered an interesting case in a young German man named Rudiger Gamm.

Rudiger was an average mathematics student at high school, but when he started work at the age of 20, he was required to do four hours of computational exercises a day. After six years,

he was able to calculate the answers to problems, such as 68 × 76, in less than five seconds. When scientists took brain scans of his thinking processes, they found he was using five more brain areas for calculating numbers than normal people do.

This case illustrates the amazing adaptability of the human brain — your brain can do the same!

Setting Recall Times

In the weeks leading up to an exam, you need to do as much consistent practical preparation as possible. This means spending a lot of time on reviewing and rewriting your new condensed study notes.

Review each subject's material and rewrite it into condensed mind maps, concept maps, essay route maps, and other visual formats, as I outline in Chapters 10 and 11, at least two weeks before your exams. That way, you can use those last two weeks to focus solely on committing your notes to memory. This entails practicing your understanding of the material through recall rehearsal (see "Working with Your Learning Styles" earlier in this chapter), and your ideal exam scenario through performance rehearsal (covered in Chapter 15).

Counting down the days

To do well, you need to establish a detailed timetable for those final two weeks before the exam, perhaps covering two subjects a day — one in the morning; one in the afternoon. Your efforts must also be consistent. Rehearsal means repetition. If you don't prepare a good review timetable and stick to it, the good results you're hoping for are less likely to show through.

In Table 14-1, I show a student's high-school timetable, plotting what subjects to study when, in relation to exam dates. You can use this example to help fill out your own timetable, whether you're at high school, university, or preparing for a career exam. I provide a blank timetable template in Appendix A.

Consider these points when you're organizing your timetable:

✔ Think about the subjects you're most confident in. Usually, these subjects require the least amount of scheduled review time. Set aside time to prepare for them further out from the exam, with a quick review a day or two before.

✔ How long you spend in each study session can be flexible and dependent on how you feel at the time. Generally, up to 50 minutes in each hour is possible, but the latest research suggests you get better results if you mix it up a bit. One study session may be 40 minutes, the next 20 minutes, the next 50 minutes, and so on. Keep in mind that lots of short bursts are more helpful than two hours without a break.

Changing locations and study topics is thought to improve your retention as well. For example, you might do 30 minutes of one subject in the library, then after a short break, do 50 minutes of another subject at home.

✔ Think about those subjects you're weaker in or you find more difficult. Obviously, you need to allocate study time for these subjects throughout your schedule (that is, if you want to bring up your grade).

✔ In the last two weeks before each exam, look for creative ways to review when you're doing something that doesn't require your full attention. For example, if you recorded your notes on an audio device, listen to them as you do the dishes or walk the dog.

I used to laminate my condensed mind maps and stick them on the shower wall. That way I could review the material and shower at the same time. (Stop laughing!)

Don't forget to look after yourself and maintain a mind–body balance. Take frequent short breaks, drink plenty of water to maintain hydration, and eat healthy snacks to keep up your energy and concentration levels (refer to Chapter 2).

Table 14-1

Sample Study Timetable — Final Weeks

Week	Monday	Tuesday	Wednesday	Thursday	Friday	Saturday	Sunday
9	7 School	8 School	9 French Classics	10 Classics Drama	11 Art History French	12 Classics Drama	13 Art History Drama
10	14 Art History DRAMA EXAM	15 Art History French	16 Classics ART HISTORY EXAM	17 Calculus Classics	18 Classics French	19 Calculus Classics	20 French Classics
11	21 French CLASSICS EXAM	22 Calculus French	23 CALCULUS EXAM	24 FRENCH EXAM	25	26 Vacation	27 Vacation

Applying the three Ps

One of the biggest difficulties many students face, particularly at university, is that new course material is still being presented in the days leading up to exams. This means you have to learn new material (and sometimes write assignments), while simultaneously reviewing material covered in the months prior. This process of juggling the new with the old can cause anxiety and overwhelm you, neither of which is conducive to good learning or studying.

To get through this final step in the review process and ensure you strike the right balance in the final days leading up to the exam, follow the three Ps — prepare, prioritize, and persevere:

- **Prepare:** You need to get yourself into the right mental and emotional state before each review session and avoid feeling overwhelmed. If you're feeling the pressure, look through Chapter 6 to use relaxation techniques to help you get back into balance.

- **Prioritize:** The most important thing to focus on in the days leading up to the exam is that your performance on the day will be a true reflection of the work you've done during the year. To get this right, ensure your studying takes priority over any last-minute course work and assignments. Sometimes assignments can be handed in after the exam.

- **Persevere:** Success in any area of your life usually comes down to perseverance — keep on keeping on — especially when the going gets tough. To get through the last few weeks before exams, you need the right state of mind. The exam performance mindset (discussed in Chapter 1) outlines the type of thinking that helps you stay on track. Having the right attitude, and knowing what drives you and what holds you back, ensures you can prepare to the best of your ability. Perseverance is the key.

If you use the three Ps as your grounding philosophy in the final days of preparation, you should be able to stay on track so that you're ready and raring to go on exam day.

Chapter 15

Rehearsing Your Performance

*Y*our brain processes and communicates information in a variety of ways. By rehearsing how to recall the information you have, you ensure that you retain the material you need to do well on an exam (refer to Chapter 14). Your ideal on-the-day performance can also be constructed ahead of time through mental rehearsal, otherwise known as *visualization*.

In this chapter, I clue you in on how to effectively use your imagination to build the neural networks required for a relaxed, confident, and highly productive exam performance. I discuss what comfort zones are from a performance psychology perspective, and how you can deliberately expand your comfort zone ahead of time, through mental rehearsal, to reduce exam anxiety and memory block.

Using Your Imagination

Think of taking an exam as giving a performance. Athletes, musicians, and actors train for peak performance, and use mental rehearsal to improve their on-the-day performances. Research now shows that mental practice can be effective for students taking exams as well.

Your brain doesn't know the difference between what's real and imagined (refer to Chapter 5). Your brain cells get busy in many of the same ways whether you actually do something or simply visualize doing it. One difference is that the strength of neural processing is lower when you visualize as opposed to taking action. Also, rehearsing something in your mind requires at least two-thirds of the same brain activity as doing something physically. The only difference is that instead of sending the signals down the spinal cord to move your muscles, the signals end up in your primary visual cortex — the part of your brain that allows you to construct visual images.

Can you imagine the potential for improved ability if you could spend time doing something repeatedly in your mind instead of having just one chance to get it right? This technique can be applied to exams! You aren't given the opportunity to actually do lots and lots of practice exams to condition your best responses, but you can practice them in your mind.

You can create real-life problem situations in your mind that may occur only once in every 12 exams you take. The reason to do that is to condition a response that overcomes the problem!

Airline pilots use simulators to rehearse problems that could occur during flights, even though they may experience the event only once during years of flying. But, should the event happen in reality, they know instinctively how to react. Such is the power of using mental rehearsal to enhance performance.

Mentally rehearsing to improve your test performance

Mental rehearsal involves making time to sit quietly, free of distractions, to vividly visualize your absolute ideal exam situation. Practice seeing yourself looking and feeling clear, calm, and confident, in control and assured of success. Later, when you take the exam in reality, you've conditioned yourself to respond just as you rehearsed in your mind.

Research conducted in the United States at the University of California by Lien Pham, Shelley E. Taylor, and others shows that two types of mental rehearsal can help students enhance their performance:

✔ **Process mental rehearsal:** This involves visualizing yourself doing all the tasks needed in the process of achieving a study goal. You see yourself sitting at a desk, reviewing your study materials, making notes, concentrating, and feeling good.

✔ **Outcome mental rehearsal:** This involves seeing the final outcome you want. You see yourself taking the exam with confidence and getting a great result.

Pham and Taylor's research shows a positive correlation between mental rehearsal and improved exam performance. Interestingly, though, process mental rehearsal alone showed greater improvement than outcome mental rehearsal or a combination of both. This may be due to students taking practical steps to improve their study habits after spending some time mentally rehearsing.

Consider how you want to think and feel as you prepare for your exams. Be clear about the results you're aiming for, and be positive. Take out a piece of blank paper and write down some keywords to summarize your thoughts. These keywords form positive affirmations that you can use to condition your subconscious mind.

The words help to generate the pictures and feelings you want, and these pictures and feelings influence your self-images. Your self-images are like a plane's autopilot. They drive your natural free-flowing behavior, which is the behavior you want to enhance when preparing for and taking exams. (To explore affirmations and your self-image, turn to Chapter 4.)

Do you have any areas of particular difficulty when preparing for or sitting exams? You can build the response to these difficulties into your list of affirmations and condition a new behavior. For example, if you find that you procrastinate when getting ready to study, try writing an affirmation to reduce this problem: "I want to do well. I expect to do well. All I need to do is get started now!"

When you say the words, try to create a mental movie of yourself in your study space, beginning to study. Try to make the image as real as possible. As you see the images, brain cells in the visual processing areas of your brain start firing. Now add positive feelings — expectation, determination, confidence, and so on. (Massive neural chemistry is released.) Repeat this a few times and you find that it's the pictures and feelings that condition your memory. The words are just the trigger to evoke these images and feelings in your mind.

Expanding your comfort zone

Your *comfort zone* is simply an idea you have stored in your memory about what you're like and what you do. When you try, or are asked, to do something that is not like you, you get a lot of uncomfortable feelings.

Imagine being asked to stand up right now and start singing your national anthem to a group of people. What thoughts go through your mind? Most people feel immediate discomfort (also called dissonance, which I describe in Chapter 4) at stepping outside their comfort zone.

When challenged to do something unfamiliar, you may experience physical anxiety symptoms — an increased heart rate, shallow breathing, and sweating palms. You may experience mental anxiety symptoms, such as mild aggression ("No way I'm doing that!"), memory loss, or confusion. All these hit you, bam! Like most people, you're a creature of habit, and habits are comfortable, right?

Ideas about yourself, or your *self-image*, tell you what you can and can't do. You've formed beliefs about what you're good at and not good at, and when you're asked to behave in a way that's not like your self-image (in this case, at the thought of singing to a crowd), you experience all kinds of negative physical and mental/emotional feedback... Your nonconscious memory is telling you through uncomfortable biofeedback to go back to the familiar — to go back to being you.

For many people, sitting in an exam room is not familiar territory — it's out of their comfort zone. This can apply doubly to adult students who've been out of the education system for a long time.

When you first started taking tests, were you nervous? As the whole environment and the procedure became familiar, did your anxiety lessen? If so, the process of taking exams enhanced your self-image so that you became more comfortable in that environment. You literally extended your comfort zone to include sitting in an exam room and taking a test.

The good news is you can extend your comfort zone deliberately without having to take a test! By using your imagination through mental rehearsal, you can practice feeling relaxed in a situation that in the past disturbed you. You can do mental rehearsal in the weeks prior to exams so that when the exam day arrives, you've been there so many times in your mind that your neural response of feeling calm and confident is conditioned in place.

In Appendix B, I provide a mental rehearsal script to help you rehearse performing well in exams. If you record this script on an audio player and listen to it repeatedly, you'll condition your memory and reduce any dissonance so that you feel comfortable when preparing for and sitting exams.

Dealing with Exam Anxiety

If exam anxiety hits, you can try two approaches to prevent it from disturbing your exam performance. One is mental, the other is physical, and you can do them separately or simultaneously. I discuss each in the next sections.

Thinking through the mental approach

Anxiety is created by how you interpret a situation. Your thoughts create anxiety and then give the anxiety meaning, rather than giving meaning to the actual situation.

If taking tests causes you excessive anxiety, ask yourself, "What do I believe that makes me feel this way?" If you can become aware of any limiting beliefs, you can then change your perception of what exams mean to you, and find a more relaxed response (refer to "Expanding your comfort zone" earlier in this chapter).

The biggest problem you may face in an exam is discovering you're outside your comfort zone. When this occurs, the stress-related chemicals in your brain (refer to Chapter 2) can shut down your recall and you may experience memory block. Implementing some relaxation techniques is the best remedy for this problem (see "Unblocking mentally and physically" later in this chapter).

Taking a physical approach

Try different relaxation exercises as offered in Chapters 5 and 6. Practice those that you can use at home during the build-up to an exam and in the exam itself.

A simple breathing technique you can use in an exam to reduce anxiety is to breathe out for longer than you breathe in, and in the middle, hold your breath for a long time. Use a ratio of 1:4:2. In other words, breathe in counting 4 seconds, hold for 16 seconds, then breathe out for 8 seconds. This is also rather energizing and gets plenty of oxygen to your brain. Try it now!

Unblocking mentally and physically

A memory block is a side effect of anxiety. The key to unlocking a blocked memory is to interrupt the thought pattern creating the blockage and to physically help your body to relax.

Take these three steps to eliminate memory block:

1. **Breathe deeply and relax as much as you can.**

   Use the affirmation, "Relax ... relax ... relax."

2. **Tell yourself, "I know this information and it's coming back to me now."**

3. **In your mind, let go of the need to have the information now and move on to another question.**

   Trust that the information will return when you're not trying so hard to remember it.

If you're still struggling to recall information, take a bathroom break, if you're allowed to, and rinse your face with cold water. Breathe deeply and use more positive affirmations — for example, "I am clear, calm, and confident!" — to help restore a feeling of calm.

When you feel your body and mind becoming calm, resume your exam in a new section, then come back to the difficult question later. You may even have a sudden recall in the middle of another related question. If so, quickly write down the key information in the planning space and come back to the earlier question after you finish the current question.

Part VI
The Part of Tens

Enjoy an additional (and free!) Part of Tens chapter online
at www.dummies.com/extras/passingexams.

In this part ...

- Explore ten simple strategies to use in order to prepare yourself on the day before your exam.
- Check out the ten top tips of things to do during an exam.
- Learn ten ways to maintain momentum between your exams.

Chapter 16

Ten Tips for Exam Day: Before the Event

*I*magine that your first exam day is looming. What are you telling yourself? What do you see or feel? Hopefully your responses to these questions are positive and affirming. If you've made use of this book, you should be feeling prepared and ready to go.

This chapter offers some practical suggestions to improve your overall mental, emotional, and physical state as you gear up for your exams.

Organize Your Equipment

It may sound obvious, but have you checked that you've got everything you need for the exam? Have you packed your bag?

I've heard many students say that when they got into their exam they discovered they'd forgotten their identification (ID), an extra pen or pencil, or their calculator. And I've seen a room full of people waiting for one person to go get their ID — crazy!

Put aside some time the night before your exam to organize everything you'll need:

- ✔ Your ID
- ✔ Stationery — pens (one spare), pencils (one spare), ruler, eraser
- ✔ Calculator (if necessary)
- ✔ A water bottle (if allowed)

Know Your Exam Time and Venue

Double-check your exam times and venues. If you're feeling stressed, it's so easy to get the venues and times mixed up.

What day is each test? Is the exam in the morning or afternoon? Some people turn up in the afternoon only to discover their exam was held earlier in the day! If you double-check this information, you won't make the same mistake.

Get a Good Night's Rest

Sleeping well before a big exam is really important. If you're feeling under-prepared, you may be very tempted to stay up late to cram that last piece of information into your head. The problem with this is that you won't feel rested on the day, and you may not perform as well as you could on the stuff you know well.

When you don't get a good night's sleep, your nervous system is strained and your mind and body don't operate with ease. Your brain may release all kinds of stress chemicals that can mess up your performance and cause memory blocks and brain freezes.

Bottom line: If you haven't done all the reviewing you wanted to by your normal bedtime the night before the exam, let it go. You don't want to compromise your results through lack of sleep. It's more important you get the sleep!

Eat Healthy, Energizing Food

Did you skip breakfast or lunch today? Did you grab a quick bite from a fast-food place? Are you downing the wrong type of drinks? I know many people who live off coffee or high-caffeine energy drinks, only to feel like a yo-yo, experiencing artificially-induced energy highs, which eventually turn into lows. This isn't conducive to good learning, studying, or recall.

Nutrition plays a major role in enhancing recall, because what you eat and drink gives your brain the energy it needs to maintain mental clarity and focus. Concentration and motivation can all be diminished from a lack of good nutrition.

 Eat a good breakfast and lunch on exam days. Supplement your food intake before the exam with extra fruit, grains, and nuts, and an energy drink that's healthy, such as a banana milkshake with vitamin-enriched supplements.

For other supplements considered brain foods, check out Chapter 2.

Use Positive Self-Talk

What you say to yourself about impending exams will have a profound effect on your overall performance. As Winston Churchill once said, "I am an optimist. It does not seem to be much use being anything else!"

To check yourself and ensure you're deliberately using positive self-talk, refer to Chapter 4. Positive self-talk helps condition seeing yourself in your ideal state for an exam, and also helps reduce any negative self-talk that might creep in when you're feeling out of your comfort zone.

Practice Your Mental Rehearsal

Coupled with positive self-talk is repeatedly seeing yourself in your mind as giving the best performance you can. See yourself standing outside that exam room, smiling and looking relaxed. See yourself walking confidently into that exam room, sitting down and starting the exam. See yourself answering multiple-choice or short-answer questions with ease. See yourself writing your essays furiously — you're smiling to yourself as your hand moves effortlessly across the page.

This kind of performance — mentally rehearsed — conditions the desired response when you face it in reality (refer to Chapter 15). It's as if your brain, not knowing the difference between what is real or imagined, thinks, "I've been here 20, 30, 40 times before with ease; this is just the same!"

Practice Relaxation Techniques

If you have some anxiety-coping strategies in place, you can regain your composure in the event that things start to go wrong. Exams can be highly stressful, and although a little stress is motivating, if you allow more to creep in, you may begin to feel anxious to the point where it's detrimental to your exam performance.

One year, a close friend of mine died the day before my first set of exams. I was pretty upset but knew the show must go on. I shelved my grief, relaxed my body and mind, got through the exam, and then let it all go. As it turned out, I got top marks for that first exam. I think my friend would have been proud.

Turn Nervousness into Excitement

When you're dealing with emotions (energy in motion), you need practical ways to control them. Someone once told me you can reduce nervousness by turning the emotion into excitement. When I thought about this, I could see how. Both emotions feel similar. Now, in my mind, whenever I'm in a situation that causes me to feel nervous, I switch it to excitement, which takes the edge off my nervousness.

Try doing the same if you're feeling nervous about your upcoming exam. As you're arriving at the exam room feeling nervous, tell yourself you're feeling excited. Try to instill the feeling of excitement. You'll be surprised how easily your nerves are replaced by a feeling of excited anticipation. Yes!

Keep to Yourself

So often students arrive at an exam room and begin discussing what they studied. Do you recognize this type of conversation:

> "Did you review XYZ? I heard there will be questions on it?"

> "No! Nobody told me we had to do that. Gee, I'm in big trouble!"

Discussing your readiness for exam topics with friends before you go in can be a major setback if it causes you to lose confidence in your preparation. The best strategy is to avoid conversations like this and to simply keep to yourself. Stay aloof and if anyone asks you about the exam, change the subject. Alternatively, arrive just before you're due to go in so you don't have time to talk to anyone.

Go For It!

In the few moments before you go into the exam room, try some techniques that can help improve your motivation and concentration:

- ✔ **Do a learning-kinesiology eye movement.** Move your eyes from side to side (left to right) for 60 seconds. This helps stimulate the neural pathways between your brain hemispheres, priming your whole brain for recall.

- ✔ **Breathe for mental clarity.** Do a breathing exercise such as the 1:4:2 technique: Breathe in for 4 seconds, hold it for 16 seconds, and breathe out for 8 seconds. Breathing relaxes your nervous system and improve your mental clarity. You can also do a breathing technique to counter memory block during the exam. (Check Chapter 15 for useful breathing routines.)

- ✔ **Relax!** Finally, in that moment when you're entering the room, focus on the subject and relax! Good preparation is the key to exam success; you can't prepare any longer so now is the time to put all those hours of preparation to work. This is the moment for you to give it your all. Don't hold back — go for it!

One final point, and this is optional. Some research suggests that students can perform better if they've had a caffeinated fizzy drink just before an exam. The caffeine in the drink gives them a boost in energy for the duration of the exam, enhancing concentration and mental clarity. (Mind you, this artificial boost doesn't last and quickly tapers off to produce a low about three hours later.)

Chapter 17

Ten Tips for the Exam — No Going Back Now!

*T*he exam is here! This is your chance to deliver all the information you've reviewed. Remember, taking a test is a performance, just like a sports, music, or drama performance: Your preparation needs to be demonstrated so people can evaluate your learning.

In this chapter, I offer ten tips to help you work through exam questions in the time allocated. Review this chapter as part of your study process prior to exams, making personal notes in the margin if you wish.

Recall Your Study Notes First

A good way to start is to spend the first ten minutes of the exam jotting down relevant points in the space provided, recalling as much of your memorized study notes as possible. This allows you to release any anxiety about your ability to recall information and focus entirely on answering the questions.

For a university-level human development exam, I organized the entire subject's keywords into the rows and columns of a spreadsheet, which I rewrote in the exam as soon as possible. It took me ten minutes. By the end of the exam, I made sure every keyword that represented larger content was used in one question or another. I got an A+.

During my studies, I discovered that one of my learning and thinking style preferences is logical and sequential. Keywords in spreadsheets are easier for me to recall than trying to recall a mind map.

If you don't know your learning style preferences, find out now — refer to Chapters 3 and 14. Then match your review sessions to the way your brain is naturally wired to think and learn.

Read Exam Questions Carefully

Read every exam question twice, just to make sure you don't misunderstand the meaning of the question.

Students often lose points in exams, not from lack of knowledge on a topic, but because they read an exam question too quickly. In their haste, they miss words that change the meaning of the question, so the answer they write is off-topic.

Avoiding this mistake is simple with careful reading.

Determine which Questions to Answer

In many exams, you're offered a variety of exam questions and can choose from a selection of topics. You must decide which questions to answer and which ones to leave. The key is to match what you've prepared to the best available question. Sometimes there's a perfect match and the decision is easy. Other times, however, there's no match and you have to try to fit what you've prepared to the best question option.

Take some time to think this through. Narrow your options down to two. Jot down your prepared keywords and analyze the exam questions individually. What words in the question best match the content of your keywords? Hopefully you'll become clear on which questions to answer.

If you still feel stuck, ask for inner guidance to find the best question to answer and then move on to another section. Come back to this tricky section later when you get some kind of inner prompting on the topic. (Check the "Identify and Answer Easy Questions First" section later in this chapter.)

Pace Yourself

One of the most common problems students face during an exam is spending too much time on one question and running out of time to answer others well. This is particularly common with exam essays.

Sometimes the amount of time you should spend on each question is written on the paper. Sometimes you have to work out the times yourself, by assessing the value of points given for each question. Write down (somewhere visible), the future time when you should be finishing a key exam question, like an essay. Then when you arrive at that time (say, in half an hour or 45 minutes), you can finish off quickly, or drop it for now. You can leave any final remarks or conclusion summaries until much later, and in the meantime move on to the next question.

In most exams, you receive more points from not quite finishing a greater number of questions as opposed to spending more time to finish a smaller number of questions.

If you're falling short of time, write "Out of time" in the margin and use bullet points to outline what you would've said if you'd had enough time. This gives your examiner the chance to see that you do know your stuff, but you just ran out of time. Again, this might give you a few extra points.

Identify and Answer Easy Questions First

When time is of the essence, it's useful to pass through your exam paper twice. First, zip through, answering all the questions you know you can answer quickly and easily. Then, go through the test a second time, answering questions that require more planning.

One potential problem that can arise using the revisit-later method is that you could actually miss a question. So make sure, before you finish, that you've answered every question.

I've heard students say, "I didn't know the answer so I left it blank." If you're truly stuck and you didn't do any preparation on the question, there may really be nothing you can do. The knowledge is simply not there. However, I've found that turning the question over to my memory and letting it go for a little while actually helps. I move on to other questions and then, when I least expect it, a suggestion on how to answer the question suddenly surfaces. I stop, go to a planning space, and jot down the idea immediately. It's not that the information isn't stored — it's just that my memory's recollection process isn't working at that moment. When I've finished all the other exam questions, I go back to that question and answer it with my new insight.

Make all Multiple-Choice Answers Count

Use these great methods to tackle multiple-choice questions:

- ✔ Go through multiple-choice questions three times. Always do the easy ones first. Then do the ones that require a bit more thought. Finally, do the ones that you can only guess at.

- ✔ Make sure you understand the question and possible answers fully. If you don't know, come back to it later — don't make a rushed response.

- ✔ Rule out the obviously wrong answers first thing. If you're still unsure, choose the answer that's most likely to be correct.

- ✔ Never leave a blank. Sometimes the longest answer is the correct one, or if there are two opposite answers, one of these will most likely be the correct answer. If you still don't know, choose "All of the above."

- ✔ Check for mismatching aspects between the question and answer, such as tenses used. The mismatched answer can then be eliminated.

- ✔ Generally, your first pick is the best answer. Don't change your first answer unless you're convinced it's wrong after further investigation.

Plan Essays before You Begin Writing

The key to writing good exam essays is to plan what you're going to write beforehand. Map your key points in a logical order in the planning space provided. (For information on writing essay route maps, see Chapter 10.)

The examiner wants to see that you've understood the question, can organize your thoughts and present them in a clear, concise, and logical manner within the time constraints.

Use these guidelines:

- ✔ Use at least ten per cent of your allocated time for planning. Do you fully understand the question? Pay attention to keywords such as *discuss, compare and contrast*, and *critically evaluate*.

- ✔ If you have more than one essay to write, do the planning for each at the same time.

- ✔ When writing, it's important to develop the structure with an introduction, body, and conclusion. If you run out of time, reduce the conclusion to a few rounding-off sentences. Make sure your writing is legible.

- ✔ Make each sentence count. A new idea is more points towards your grade, so the more new and relevant ideas you include, the better.

✔ Answer every essay question. Even if you're not really sure about it, guess! Try to write something relevant. Your answer could be the difference between different grade levels.

✔ If you run out of time, or you have only a few minutes remaining, skip the conclusion and review your entire paper instead. Just make sure you've summarized all the key points. Even bulleted key points are worth writing.

Take Regular, Quick Breaks

Exam hours are a time of intense mental concentration. In order to maintain your focus and pace, you need to give your body and mind moments of rest. Every 30 minutes or in brief moments between sections, take a quick break to rest your body. Do a little relaxation exercise — take a deep breath in and then, as you breathe out, tell yourself to relax. You could also use the 1:4:2 breathing technique: breathing in for 4 seconds, holding it for 16 seconds and breathing out for 8 seconds. (This breathing technique can also help if you suddenly encounter a memory block or begin to feel anxious — refer to Chapter 15.)

Sip water to keep yourself hydrated. Remember, your blood carries oxygen and nutrients to your brain. Blood is 83 percent water. Lack of water can lead to a lack of concentration (see Chapter 2).

After your rest break, when you're ready to begin again, set your intent for the next period of prolonged concentration, clarity, and focus. You can do it!

Ask for Divine Help

Whatever your religious or spiritual beliefs, your own personal unseen forces can help you in an exam.

I remember going into an exam with a classmate who had not prepared. She said, "God help me!" And, it seems, God did. Whether she drew on divine inspiration or not, I don't know, but somehow she passed the exam with an above-average grade. I have also heard stories from students who claim they use their imagination to talk to their teacher in their head when they don't know an answer.

In some ways, imagining that someone else is with you is like turning the problem over to your nonconscious memory to find the answer. If it's true that all your experiences are recorded in your memory at various levels of recollection, then the answer may be there too! A technique such as asking for help — from God or your teacher — could be like probing your memory to deliver an answer. I don't know for sure, but if it works, why not try it?

Review Your Answers — Don't Leave Early!

If you finish an exam early, make use of the extra time to review your answers. Tidy up any spelling errors or messy writing. Look at those questions you found more difficult. Can you add anything to your answers?

Taking a few moments to review your paper may help you discover that overlooked question you planned to come back to later and forgot about.

Don't leave early. Don't forget that your exam is a performance and you only have one shot at it. You might as well use all your time wisely.

Chapter 18

Ten Ways to Maintain Momentum between Exams

As the saying goes, "It ain't over till it's over!" You can adopt this kind of attitude to spur yourself on until you finish all your exams. Try to ride that momentum for as long as you can — preferably until you walk out of the exam room after your last exam. Only then can you really let go.

In this chapter, I offer ten ideas to help you maintain momentum and keep your life in balance as you complete one exam after another.

Staying Balanced

If your exams span several weeks, try to keep a balanced lifestyle throughout the process. Yes, your exams are important to you, but you need to maintain a bigger perspective. That way you'll be able to last the distance *and* avoid causing problems in other areas of your life.

I'll always remember how much I annoyed my girlfriend (who later became my wife), when I was preparing for my university exams. I was so focused on wanting to do well that I often neglected her. Because I wasn't giving much time to our relationship during exams, she was ready to walk out. I realized after that I had to look at my priorities. Yes, the exams were important, but so were my relationships and my work. I changed my perspective to keeping the balance and have retained that perspective to this day.

Ask yourself, "What's the worst thing that can happen to me if everything goes wrong? Will this be the end of the world as I know it? Will I get another chance?" If you enlarge your perspective, your priorities will become clearer and the task ahead of you easier.

Being Relaxed

You need to be motivated and active during the days between your exams, but that doesn't mean you can't rest. By all means, rest when you need to, but do it with intent, not because you failed to set a goal.

For some ideas on how to rest with intent, and also how to stay relaxed so that you don't become stressed during this busy time, refer to Chapters 5 and 6.

Planning Rewards After Each Exam

Creating a positive reward or treat for yourself after each exam can increase your motivation. Make a contract with yourself: "Okay, after I get this history exam out of the way I'll give myself the night off to go to that movie with Jenny."

Making a commitment like this keeps you motivated throughout the exam process. Committed, you're less likely to engage in procrastination or other creative-avoidance strategies. Doing the next exam becomes a "want to" instead of a "have to." (For more ways to maintain motivation, refer to Chapter 3.)

Keeping Your Eye on Upcoming Exams

Your daily and weekly review schedule should allot time to prepare for all your exam subjects. If some subjects require more effort than others, schedule more time for them (refer to Chapter 14).

You probably won't be able to schedule enough time to prepare new material between exams, so you need to concentrate on preparing for all your exams before the first one starts. During the exam weeks, your study sessions should primarily focus on practicing your understanding of the subject content and rehearsing your recall.

Start thinking about preparing for your second exam before the first exam has started. This helps keep your mind engaged and working for you. You keep the energy, motivation, and drive happening. Otherwise, as soon as you finish your first exam, your energy will shut off.

Ensuring Comparisons Don't Erode Your Confidence

If friends ask questions about what you did in the exam, try to avoid answering them directly. The reason for this is that after you start comparing what you did with someone else, you may suddenly realize where you may have gone wrong. This can be quite damaging to your confidence, motivation, and general morale, and affect how you perform in subsequent exams.

This kind of scenario can be likened to Olympic athletes who mess up during a performance. Have you seen how they carry on regardless, but their energy has dropped slightly? They know they cannot win.

Performance psychology is such a mind game. For example, if you're discussing the details of an exam with a friend and you discover you messed up, the feedback can really hold you back on your upcoming exams. Without knowing, the disappointment can cause reduced energy and drive, and tempt you to various avoidance strategies. You're better off saying nothing until after your last exam is over.

If you do discuss and compare your performance with others between exams, you'll need to talk yourself up again (through affirmations, covered in Chapter 4) and get back on the horse!

Reorganizing Your Preparation Time

Your preparation time planner (see Appendix A) needs to be flexible as you finish one exam and move on to another. Be prepared to make amendments. For example, you may find that having done one exam, the time you've allocated to prepare for the next exam is long enough to also prepare for the third exam. However, if your fourth exam, your hardest subject, occurs the day after your third exam, allocate it more review time between your second and third exams.

Take some time to really think about what you need to prepare and when. And as you complete exams, fine-tune your timetable to accommodate your subject strengths and weaknesses. These are aspects that often evolve as you progress through your schedule.

Going to Bed Early

Even if you feel under-prepared between exams, you're better off finishing what you can and going to bed at your normal time.

Your exam-day performance will suffer if you're tired from staying up all night studying. Go to bed early!

Maintaining Your Mental Rehearsal

Prepare a mental rehearsal script to listen to over and over, as I explain in Chapter 15. If you haven't recorded your script yet, get it recorded as soon as possible and use it before each exam. (Appendix B has a sample script.)

Before you go to sleep at night, listen to the script. Use affirmative statements to help see yourself in your next exam. See yourself walking confidently into that exam room, feeling calm and knowing you have what it takes to do well in this exam. Tell yourself, "This is it and I am ready!" See yourself writing furiously and feeling excited and answering every question easily. Run through this performance rehearsal as you go off to sleep. When you first wake up in the morning, listen to it again.

As you imprint your memory in this way, you'll notice the same response when you walk into that exam room. If you've mentally rehearsed well, you'll feel what you felt in your imagined experience of it. Well done!

Celebrating Your Completed Exam (s)

As your final exams loom, you'll see the light at the end of the tunnel! Begin thinking about what you'd like to do to pat yourself on the back for all the hard work you put in. This is important, for research shows that people often pass over their successes too quickly.

Even before you get your results, really wallow in the positive feelings that make you feel good about yourself. This helps build your self-image, improving your self-efficacy and self-esteem (more on these topics in Chapter 4).

Celebrate all your hard work, whatever the outcome. If you know you've given it your best shot, then you can ask nothing more of yourself except to relax and have fun for a little while.

Celebrating all your hard work after exams is great fun, but go easy. Don't drink and drive, or do anything stupid. The cost is too high!

This isn't a happy story, but I believe it's important to relate because it happens all too often. When I was at high school, a group of top students planned a post-exam party. Tragically, the celebration got out of hand and while driving home, the group had a car accident. One of the school's top all-round students was killed, the others badly hurt. The accident was a devastating blow to the families, friends, and the school.

Getting Your Life Back!

Whether you're at high school, university, or undertaking career exams, when they're over, they're over! Get your life back to normal and enjoy your free time. Catch up on all those not-so-important things you put aside. Make time to meet up with friends, play sports, and socialize. Get out in nature — you deserve it. Well done!

Part VII
Appendixes

In this part ...

- Schedule your workload with a daily planner and weekly planner template.

- Discover relaxation scripts you can use to help you relax and prepare for exams.

- Use a learning quiz to discover your natural way of learning and the areas you could improve.

Appendix A

Planners

. . . .

*U*se the daily planner and weekly planner in this appendix to schedule your workload.

Your daily planner helps you to prioritize the important things you want to achieve throughout each day. Prioritizing is the key to turning your "to do" list into a "stay on track" list. All those little tasks you identify as important to do each day, in time, help you realize your greater goals.

Your daily planner can contain a variety of goals — go to a friend's house for dinner, buy the groceries, take out the trash, finish your assignment, and so on. Although each goal is important, placing an A, B, or C in the P (Priority) column next to each helps you see your most important tasks easily and helps you schedule the time you have available. After you schedule your A tasks, go on to B and C tasks. Use the C (Completed) column to mark your accomplishments.

Use the weekly planner to split each day into goals you want to accomplish each morning and afternoon/evening. The open format gives the appearance of having more time and helps you decide how much time to allocate to each task and where in the week it fits best.

Note: A weekly planner is particularly useful in the final few weeks prior to exams. By noting down the time allotted to review each subject, you can see precisely what to review and when. Make sure you allocate more time to those subjects you feel less confident about.

Your smart phone probably has a calendar/event planning feature. You can also find a variety of time planners online. Check out Day Viewer at www.dayviewer.com, or, for a price, you can use Smart Sheet at www.smartsheet.com.

DAILY PLANNER

TIME SCHEDULE	P	ACTIVITY	C
7 a.m.			
8 a.m.			
9 a.m.			
10 a.m.			
11 a.m.			
12 noon			
1 p.m.			
2 p.m.			
3 p.m.			
4 p.m.			
5 p.m.			
6 p.m.			
7 p.m.			
8 p.m.			
9 p.m.			
10 p.m.			

P = Priority (allocate a letter in order of importance)

C = Completed

WEEKLY PLANNER

	SUNDAY	MONDAY	TUESDAY	WEDNESDAY	THURSDAY	FRIDAY	SATURDAY
a.m.							
p.m.							

Appendix B

Relaxation and Visualization Scripts

• •

*T*his appendix provides scripts you can use to help you relax and prepare for exams. Record them to an audio device so that you can listen to them often. When recording, use a slow, firm voice and, if possible, play classical baroque music in the background. Listen to scripts before you go to sleep at night, when you're riding in the car — not while you're driving! — or any other time that's convenient.

For more information on applying these scripts, refer to Chapter 5.

Relaxation Script

Time: 3 minutes

[Insert your name], close your eyes and begin to breathe deeply ... Breathe in through your nose and out through your mouth. With every exhale, imagine any tension in your body going out with it. I'm going to count from five to one, and as I do, you will feel yourself relaxing with every descending number. At number one, you will be totally relaxed, yet alert to what I'm saying.

[Insert your name], I am counting now. Five, you're beginning to relax ... Four, breathe deeply, let go. Three, begin to get a sense of your body, the position of your arms and hands, the position of your legs and feet — feel your weight in the chair. Two, continuing down ... One, you're totally relaxed, and you quietly repeat to yourself, "Relax ... relax ... relax ...." Feel yourself letting go of any tension in your body. You are now totally relaxed, [insert your name], yet totally alert.

Rest in this state for a moment, breathing deeply and affirming the words, "Relax ... relax ... relax." This is alpha state.

Now, I am going to ask you to anchor this feeling in your body by touching the thumb and first finger of your right hand together. Do this now. As you feel this relaxed state, bring your thumb and first finger together. Repeat this sequence several times, feeling relaxed and bringing your fingers together. From now on, whenever you want to bring yourself into this relaxed state quickly, as soon as you put your thumb and first finger together, this feeling of relaxation will begin to come over you. This gesture is your trigger to help this relaxed feeling start to come over you. Know that as soon as you bring your thumb and first finger together, you will begin to feel relaxed.

In a moment, I am going to count from one to five. When I reach five, you will open your eyes and return to the room, feeling totally at ease. One, you feel yourself come up. Two, coming up ... Three, coming up ... Four, beginning to open your eyes ... Five, you're fully awake now, alert and at ease. Smile.

Mental Rehearsal Script

Time: 10 minutes

This script takes advantage of research into how your mind works and mental rehearsal. Have someone read this to you, or read it yourself while audio-recording it for later use. Read the entire script very slowly in a low, firm voice.

The script has three parts. First, you're going to relax for three minutes, using part of the preceding relaxation script. Then, you're going to create your ideal process rehearsal script. This also takes about three minutes. The final stage in this script is creating your ideal outcome rehearsal script. This takes about four minutes.

Relax first

[Insert your name], close your eyes and begin to breathe deeply, in through your nose and out through your mouth. With every exhale, imagine any tension in your body going out with your breath. I am going to count from five to one, and as I do, you will feel yourself relaxing with every descending number. When you reach number one, you will be totally relaxed, yet alert to what I am saying.

[Insert your name], I am counting now. Five, you're beginning to relax ... Four, breathe deeply, let go. Three, begin to get a sense of your body, the position of your arms and hands, the position of your legs and feet — feel your weight in the chair. Two, continuing down ... One, you're totally relaxed and you quietly repeat to yourself, "Relax ... relax ... relax ...." Feel yourself letting go of any tension in your body. You are now totally relaxed, [insert your name], yet totally alert.

Rest in this state for a moment — this is alpha state.

Ideal process script

First, I want you to imagine yourself at your study desk or the place you tend to study and review. See yourself sitting there with everything you need around you — class notes, pens, blank paper, a bottle or glass of water. See yourself with your eyes closed, and feel yourself relaxing as you enter alpha state. You can hear soft music playing in the background. Feel alpha state now.

In your mind's eye, [insert your name], see yourself open your eyes and sit up. Say to yourself, "I am ready to review. I will hold my full attention to this task for the next 50 minutes."

Now see yourself begin to look through your notes, reviewing material and rewriting these in condensed formats. See yourself totally absorbed as you work effortlessly through this review session. Feel yourself focused, energized, determined. Say to yourself, "I'm on a roll. This is easy ...." Smile.

Ideal outcome script

[Insert your name], imagine yourself moving forward in time to the day of your first exam. See yourself looking calm and confident. You are walking into the exam room, and you are feeling relaxed, because you know you have done your best to prepare.

Choose a seat in the room. Are you at the front, in the middle, or at the back of the room? Are you to the left or right? Sit down and smile at your friends around you.

Take a deep breath. Relax and say to yourself, "This is it! Everything I need, I have within me now." Smile.

See the examiner giving instruction to the group. Now see yourself starting the test and looking through it.

See yourself smiling because you've prepared for these exact questions. You put your head down and begin writing. Say to yourself, "I am clear, calm, and confident. Everything I need to write is coming to me now." Feel a sense of calm certainty that you're doing your very best. All your preparation is being used for this moment.

Now move forward in time to the end of the exam. You've finished writing with time to spare and you're looking through your answers to see whether if there's anything you can improve on. Feel yourself relax, [insert your name], as the exam is finishing. Feel satisfied with what you have done. Smile and say, "Okay, bring on the next test."

Now move forward in time to receiving your grades. You stand there holding the envelope (or sit looking at the computer). You tear open the envelope (or look at the web page) and find that you've reached your goals, and in some subjects done better than you thought. Smile and say, "Yes!"

In a moment, I am going to count from one to five. When I reach five, you will open your eyes and return to the room, feeling totally at ease. One, you feel yourself come up. Two, coming up ... Three, coming up ... Four, beginning to open your eyes ... Five, you're fully awake now, alert and at ease. Smile.

Appendix C

Learning Style Quiz and Motivational Reminder

· ·

*U*se the Learning Style Quiz in this appendix to discover your natural way of learning and the areas you aren't so strong in. You can then work on developing your weak learning areas so that you're never at a disadvantage.

For more information on learning styles, refer to Chapters 3 and 14. I also provide additional resources on my website, www.passingexams.co.nz.

This appendix also includes a little poster you can photocopy to help keep you motivated.

Learning Style Quiz

Take this quick quiz by circling the letter(s) next to the answer that most applies to you. Answer each question as honestly as you can. At the end, add up your scores to get a basic idea of your dominant learning style.

If a friend asked you how to find a particular place, how would you give her directions?

> **V:** Quickly draw her a map.
>
> **A:** Casually tell her how to get there.
>
> **K:** Take her by the hand and guide her.
>
> **An:** Logically explain her best path, step by step.

If you bought a new car, what would influence your decision the most?

   V: It looks really good.

   A: It has a great sound system.

   K: It feels really comfortable to sit in.

   An: You've worked out that it's a good deal and will save you money in the long run.

How do you usually learn to use a new piece of technology?

   V: Watch someone else do it first.

   A: Get someone to explain it.

   K: Jump straight in and just do it.

   An: Read the instructions and carefully work it out.

When you go to a movie, what impresses you the most?

   V: The great visual effects and cinematography.

   A: The awesome sound track.

   K: How comfortable the seats are.

   An: The technical mastery behind the scenes.

How do you prefer a teacher to give information?

   V: Use overheads, hand-outs, notes.

   A: Discuss the topic in the classroom.

   K: Go on field trips that offer hands-on experience.

   An: Analyze and problem-solve topics.

When you have forgotten how to spell a word, what do you do most often?

   V: Try to see it in your mind's eye.

   A: Try to sound it out.

   K: Write down both versions that come to mind and then work it out.

   An: Get a dictionary.

In your spare time, what are you most likely to do?

    V: Do art, painting, photography.

    A: Listen to music; play an instrument.

    K: Play sports, jog, swim.

    An: Read, write, do crossword or Sudoku puzzles.

What is your preferred method of remembering?

    V: Doing drawings or diagrams.

    A: Recording information and listening to it.

    K: Acting or rehearsing the information.

    An: Analyzing the information, conceptualizing it, problem solving.

How do you really know when someone likes you?

    V: When they show you, through gifts.

    A: When they affirm you being you.

    K: When they're physically affectionate and give you kisses and hugs.

    An: When you know they understand you.

How do you normally show someone you like them?

    V: Show them through gifts and doing things for them.

    A: Tell them when the opportunity arises.

    K: Show physical affection — kisses and hugs.

    An: Let them know you understand them.

The letter you circled most often indicates your preferred style of learning: V = Visual, A = Auditory, K = Kinesthetic (movement/feeling), An = Analytical.

Stay Motivated!

Use this cartoon to inspire yourself and stay on target when you're studying. Photocopy it and post it in your study area, or in different areas around your house.

Index

code words, for interrupting
     limiting thought patterns, 72
cognitive dissonance and change, 69
comfort zone, expanding, 188–189
comparisons and confidence
     erosion, 209–210
comprehension, testing, 125–126
concentration
   maintaining, 59–60, 111
   ruining, 70
   shortcut to, 96–97
concept maps, 133–138
concerts, active and passive, 95
conditioned beliefs, 68
conscious competence, 41
conscious incompetence, 41
conscious mind, perceiving with, 65
corpus callosum, strengthening
     through juggling, 40–41
cortex, 23

• D •

daily body rhythms, 49–50
daily planner, 215, 216
Day Viewer website, 215
declaration memory, 67
delta waves, 34
dendrites, 23, 25
Dennison, Paul and Gail, 40
Diagram World (Microsoft Word), 133
diencephalon, 24
distracted, effect of being, 70
distraction scale, use of, 47–48
distractions
   effect on concentration, 60
   eliminating, 46–47
   managing, 60
divine help, asking for, 204–205
Doidge, Norman, 36
dopamine, 149

• E •

eating before exams, 195
Ebbinghaus curve, 152
Ebbinghaus, Hermann, 152

Educational Kinesiology, 40
effort in learning, 28, 32
emotion, in memorizing, 146–147,
     149–150
emotions
   engaging, 32–33
   in learning, 28
   releasing unwanted, 101–102
environment, effect on
     concentration, 59
episodic memory, 67
essay content for exams,
     remembering, 172–174
essay route maps, 138–142
essays, planning before writing,
     203–204
exam essay content, remembering
     for easy recall, 172–174
exam nerves website, 177
exam performance mindset,
     developing, 10–12
exams
   answering easy questions, 202
   answering multiple-choice
     questions, 202–203
   careful reading of questions, 200
   dealing with anxiety, 189–190
   knowing time and venue, 194
   obtaining copies of past year's,
     115–116
   reviewing answers in, 205
   taking breaks in, 204
exercise
   effect on brain function, 38
   for relaxation, 94
explicit memory, 67
explicit value, 56
external distractions, reducing,
     46–47
eye contact in review classes, 116
eye-movement exercise, 40

• F •

facial expressions in review classes,
     116–117
facts, taking in, 124

procedural memory, 67
process mental rehearsal, 187
process visualization, 82
procrastination
  effect of, 70
  overcoming, 57–59
  three-step reduction strategy, 58
psychological learning
    implications of synaptic
    connections, 27
purpose, setting, 11

• Q •

questions in exam
  reading carefully, 200
  which to answer, 200–201
quick-relax technique, 97

• R •

reading speed, testing, 128
reading techniques, 121–128
reading white on black, 120
recall, rehearsing for, 18–19
recall times, setting, 181–184
recency effect in memory,
    152–153
reflector personalities, 55
relaxation
  before exams, 196
  between exams, 208
  in exam preparation, 16
  exercising for, 94
  in paying attention, 29
  shortcut to, 96
relaxation script, 219–220
repetition in memorizing, 147
retention, improving by reviewing
    information, 33
review classes, paying attention at,
    116–117
reviewing exam answers, 205
rewards
  after each exam, 208
  for motivation purposes, 48

rhyme creation for memorization,
    159
Richards, Ian, "Leading From the
    Inside", 122–123
roadblocks, clearing, 11–12
Robbins, Anthony, 91
Rose, Colin, 88
rote learning
  effect of, 26
  process, 155–163
rubber band technique, 72

• S •

Scheele, Paul, 128
science formulas, memorizing, 172
Sedona Method of emotional
    release, 101
seeing, effect of conditioning on,
    68–69
segmented intent website, 111
self, memory of, 67–71
self-belief
  effect on perception and
    experience, 69
  and success, 56
self-defeating problems,
    identifying, 58
self-efficacy beliefs, 73
self-esteem, enhancing, 73–74
self-hypnosis (autosuggestion),
    89–91
self-image
  influence of self-talk on, 15
  maintenance of, 71
self-pacing in exams, 201
self-sabotage, dealing with,
    11–12
self-talk
  effect of, 64, 70
  improving, 71–74
  listening to, 15
semantic memory, 67
senses
  involvement of, 31–32
  in learning, 28
short-term memory, 151

About the Author

Patrick Sherratt works as an author, speaker and trainer across the Asia Pacific region teaching individuals and organizations a synthesis of both meta-cognitive knowledge (learning how to learn), and performance psychology: visit www.passingexams.co.nz.

Having come from a farming background in rural New Zealand where academic achievement was not a high expectation, Patrick did not pursue academic goals until his late 20s when he studied psychology through Massey University. His interest in learning was transformed and throughout his degree he received many A grades. This was rewarded in 2000, when Patrick won one of the university's highest academic awards for excellence.

After completing his undergraduate degree in psychology in 2001, Patrick began teaching communication and study skills at Eastern Institute of Technology (EIT), while completing his masters degree in education. In 2008, after completing his masters, Patrick left EIT and co-founded an independent consultancy and training business called Innervate (Ltd): visit www.innervate.co.nz.

As an author, Patrick has written a number of educational resources for students, parents, and teachers. He has also produced a range of educational videos as part of a multi-media teaching resource: visit www.cliview.com.au for more information. *Passing Exams For Dummies* is his fifth book.

Patrick has been interviewed on both New Zealand and Australian radio and television and also regularly presents at international conferences. Clips from Patrick's presentations can be seen on his YouTube Channel: www.youtube.com/user/patricksherratt.

Author's Acknowledgements

The creative manifestation process is magical. From simply an idea, this collection of pages you hold has become a physical reality. And yet, they're really just a bunch of words and illustrations that hold little value unless you take them and turn them into practical and, hopefully, successful results.

Many people have been involved in the construction of the second edition of this book, all of whom I bet would really like to see you do well in your exams (otherwise all their hard work will be in vain). Do you feel the pressure now?

To acknowledge them for you, I thank my wife, Leigh, and my children Luis, Ella, and Nicolas, who gave me the time and space to write the text. I also want to thank the design and publishing teams at John Wiley & Sons in Brisbane and Melbourne, and especially the head of this project Clare Dowdell, project editor Dani Karvess, and editor Kathleen Dobie, for taking my thoughts and organizing them into a user-friendly manuscript.

Finally, I would like to acknowledge *you*, for without your desire to improve your exam results, I would never have found any reason for writing this book in the first place!

I wish you all the academic success you are seeking. Make it so!

Publisher's Acknowledgements

We're proud of this book; please send us your comments through our online registration form located at dummies.custhelp.com.

Some of the people who helped bring this book to market include the following:

Acquisitions, Editorial, and Media Development

Project Editor: Kathleen Dobie

Acquisitions Editor: Clare Dowdell

Editorial Manager: Dani Karvess

Production

Graphics: diacriTech

Proofreader: Kerry Laundon

Indexer: Don Jordan, Antipodes Indexing

The author and publisher would like to thank the following copyright holders, organisations and individuals for their permission to reproduce copyright material in this book:

- **Figure 2-1, page 23:** Getty Images/Science Photo Library/Mark Thomas
- **Figure 9-1, pages 122 and 123:** Richards, I.C (richardsi@innervate.co.nz), (2006), 'Leading from the inside', NZ Principal, March 2006. Reproduced with permission.

Every effort has been made to trace the ownership of copyright material. Information that enables the publisher to rectify any error or omission in subsequent editions is welcome. In such cases, please contact the Legal Services section of John Wiley & Sons Australia, Ltd.

Notes

Notes

Notes

Math & Science

Algebra I
For Dummies,
2nd Edition
978-0-470-55964-2

Anatomy and
Physiology
For Dummies,
2nd Edition
978-0-470-92326-9

Astronomy
For Dummies,
3rd Edition
978-1-118-37697-3

Biology
For Dummies,
2nd Edition
978-0-470-59875-7

Chemistry
For Dummies,
2nd Edition
978-1-1180-0730-3

Pre-Algebra
Essentials
For Dummies
978-0-470-61838-7

Microsoft Office

Excel 2013
For Dummies
978-1-118-51012-4

Office 2013 All-in-
One For Dummies
978-1-118-51636-2

PowerPoint 2013
For Dummies
978-1-118-50253-2

Word 2013
For Dummies
978-1-118-49123-2

Music

Blues Harmonica
For Dummies
978-1-118-25269-7

Guitar For Dummies,
3rd Edition
978-1-118-11554-1

iPod & iTunes
For Dummies,
10th Edition
978-1-118-50864-0

Programming

Android Application
Development
For Dummies,
2nd Edition
978-1-118-38710-8

iOS 6 Application
Development
For Dummies
978-1-118-50880-0

Java For Dummies,
5th Edition
978-0-470-37173-2

Religion & Inspiration

The Bible
For Dummies
978-0-7645-5296-0

Buddhism
For Dummies,
2nd Edition
978-1-118-02379-2

Catholicism
For Dummies,
2nd Edition
978-1-118-07778-8

Self-Help & Relationships

Bipolar Disorder
For Dummies,
2nd Edition
978-1-118-33882-7

Meditation
For Dummies,
3rd Edition
978-1-118-29144-3

Seniors

Computers
For Seniors
For Dummies,
3rd Edition
978-1-118-11553-4

iPad For Seniors
For Dummies,
5th Edition
978-1-118-49708-1

Smartphones & Tablets

Android Phones
For Dummies
978-1-118-16952-0

Kindle Fire HD
For Dummies
978-1-118-42223-6

NOOK HD
For Dummies,
Portable Edition
978-1-118-39498-4

Surface
For Dummies
978-1-118-49634-3

Windows 8

Windows 8
For Dummies
978-1-118-13461-0

Windows 8
For Dummies,
Book + DVD Bundle
978-1-118-27167-4

Windows 8 All-in-On
For Dummies
978-1-118-11920-4

Available in print and e-book formats.

Take Dummies with you everywhere you go!

Whether you're excited about e-books, want more from the web, must have your mobile apps, or swept up in social media, Dummies makes everything easier .